U.S. NUCLEAR WEAPONS IN EUROPE

JEFFREY RECORD *with the assistance of Thomas I. Anderson*

U.S. NUCLEAR WEAPONS IN EUROPE

Issues and Alternatives

THE BROOKINGS INSTITUTION
Washington, D.C.

Library of Congress Cataloging in Publication Data:
Record, Jeffrey.
U. S. nuclear weapons in Europe.
(Studies in defense policy)
Includes bibliographical references.
1.   North Atlantic Treaty Organization—United States.
2.   Atomic weapons.   3.   United States—Military policy.
I.   Anderson, Thomas I., joint author.   II.   Title.
III.   Series.
UA646.5.U5R42   355.03'3573   74-23433
ISBN 0-8157-7365-X

9 8 7 6 5 4 3 2 1

THE BROOKINGS INSTITUTION is an independent organization devoted to nonpartisan research, education, and publication in economics, government, foreign policy, and the social sciences generally. Its principal purposes are to aid in the development of sound public policies and to promote public understanding of issues of national importance.

The Institution was founded on December 8, 1927, to merge the activities of the Institute for Government Research, founded in 1916, the Institute of Economics, founded in 1922, and the Robert Brookings Graduate School of Economics and Government, founded in 1924.

The Board of Trustees is responsible for the general administration of the Institution, while the immediate direction of the policies, program, and staff is vested in the President, assisted by an advisory committee of the officers and staff. The by-laws of the Institution state, "It is the function of the Trustees to make possible the conduct of scientific research, and publication, under the most favorable conditions, and to safeguard the independence of the research staff in the pursuit of their studies and in the publication of the results of such studies. It is not a part of their function to determine, control, or influence the conduct of particular investigations or the conclusions reached."

The President bears final responsibility for the decision to publish a manuscript as a Brookings book or staff paper. In reaching his judgment on the competence, accuracy, and objectivity of each study, the President is advised by the director of the appropriate research program and weighs the views of a panel of expert outside readers who report to him in confidence on the quality of the work. Publication of a work signifies that it is deemed to be a competent treatment worthy of public consideration; such publication does not imply endorsement of conclusions or recommendations contained in the study.

The Institution maintains its position of neutrality on issues of public policy in order to safeguard the intellectual freedom of the staff. Hence interpretations or conclusions in Brookings publications should be understood to be solely those of the author or authors and should not be attributed to the Institution, to its trustees, officers, or other staff members, or to the organizations that support its research.

FOREWORD

The maintenance of U.S. forces in Europe has been a subject of controversy in the United States for many years. The general issue—the political purposes served by the U.S. military presence, the likelihood of conflict, and the equitable sharing of costs—was treated in an earlier Brookings book, *U.S. Troops in Europe: Issues, Costs, and Choices* (1971), by John Newhouse with Melvin Croan, Edward R. Fried, and Timothy W. Stanley. The more specific question of whether the military structure of U.S. general purpose forces in NATO is properly adapted to the threat posed by the Soviet Union and its Warsaw Pact allies was subsequently explored by Richard D. Lawrence and Jeffrey Record in the 1974 Brookings publication, *U.S. Force Structure in NATO: An Alternative.*

Jeffrey Record, assisted by Thomas I. Anderson, argues here that the present U.S. deployment of tactical nuclear weapons in the European area confers few if any net military advantages on the Atlantic Alliance, although it is politically important to America's European allies. His assessment of Soviet tactical nuclear weapons and doctrine reveals a force designed for massive and relatively indiscriminate employment; in contrast, the American tactical nuclear posture, based largely on the dubious hypothesis of NATO first use, reflects preparation for selective tactical nuclear war, which the author considers a remote prospect. He proposes major changes in the size and character of the present deployment as well as in the doctrine that governs its use.

Dissatisfaction with the present U.S. tactical nuclear posture in Europe is growing both in the Congress and in the Department of Defense, so that some of the issues and proposals addressed in this study are not new, although their importance to the future disposition of U.S. military power on the continent is undiminished.

Jeffrey Record is a research associate and Rockefeller Younger

Scholar on the defense analysis staff of the Brookings Foreign Policy Studies program, which is directed by Henry Owen. Major Thomas I. Anderson of the U.S. Air Force was a Federal Executive Fellow at the Brookings Institution in 1973-74.

The Brookings Institution thanks Dennis M. Gormley, Morton H. Halperin, John Newhouse, George H. Quester, General Matthew B. Ridgway, and Major General W. Y. Smith for their helpful comments on this study. The author is also grateful for the suggestions of his Brookings colleagues Barry M. Blechman, Edward R. Fried, Alton H. Quanbeck, Henry Owen, and Archie L. Wood; to Ellen A. Ash, who edited the manuscript; to Christine Lipsey, who checked the data and references; and to Deborah Kinsey, who typed it.

The Institution also acknowledges the assistance of the Ford Foundation, whose grant helps to support its defense and foreign policy studies. The views expressed here are those of the author and should not be ascribed to those who commented on the study, to the Ford Foundation, or to the trustees, officers, or other staff members of the Brookings Institution.

KERMIT GORDON
President

October 1974
Washington, D.C.

CONTENTS

GLOSSARY

ADM Atomic demolition munitions

AEC Atomic Energy Commission

CEP Circular error probable

DPC Defense Planning Committee

dual-capable Capable of delivering both conventional and nuclear ordnance

FBS Forward-based system(s)

GSP General Strike Plan

IOC Initial operational capability

MBFR Mutual and balanced force reductions

MIRV Multiple independently targetable reentry vehicles(s)

MR/IRBM Medium- and intermediate-range ballistic missile(s)

NATO North Atlantic Treaty Organization

NATO Europe European member states of the North Atlantic Treaty Organization

PAL Permissive Action Link

QRA Quick Reaction Alert

SACEUR Supreme Allied Commander Europe

SAM Surface-to-air missile(s)

SHAPE Supreme Headquarters Allied Powers Europe

SSM Surface-to-Surface missile(s)

TNW Tactical nuclear weapon(s)

USAREUR United States Army Europe

CHAPTER ONE

INTRODUCTION

A policy of greater reliance on tactical nuclear weapons for both deterrence and defense in Europe is receiving increasing attention in the United States today. More and more observers contend that the emergence of strategic parity between the United States and the Soviet Union, on the one hand, and spiraling manpower costs, mounting congressional demands for U.S. force reductions on the continent, and declining Western European defense budgets, on the other, have eroded the credibility of all of NATO's potential responses to aggression except that involving tactical nuclear weapons (TNW). Under NATO's strategy of flexible response, the functions of TNW are to reinforce the credibility of the U.S. strategic deterrent and, if necessary, to supplement conventional defense of Western Europe. Coincident with these pressures for a nuclear defense is a widespread dissatisfaction with present U.S. tactical nuclear posture in Europe. That posture, based on weapons and doctrine developed for the most part in the late 1950s and early 1960s, is thought by many to be unsuited for the current requirements of either deterrence or defense. Pressures for a nuclear defense of Europe are, therefore, often accompanied by demands for changes in both strategy and hardware.

The purpose of this study is to investigate the present tactical nuclear posture of the United States in NATO, including its underlying rationale, and to set forth a number of alternatives. Particular attention is paid to current proposals that would change the basic character of the U.S. TNW deployment in Europe. The military, political, and, where possible, budgetary consequences of each alternative are analyzed.

In Chapter 2 an attempt is made to construct a workable definition of TNW, followed in Chapter 3 by an assessment of the rationales behind the U.S. deployment in Europe. Chapter 4 surveys the character, capabilities, costs, and missions of the U.S. deployment, as well as allied capabilities. Chapter 5 identifies and discusses the asymmetries between U.S. and Soviet tactical nuclear postures that have implications for the kind of tactical nuclear war envisaged by U.S. strategists. Weaknesses in the present U.S. posture are assessed in Chapter 6.

Chapter 7 presents four alternatives to the current posture. The first essentially retains the present posture, but with substantially fewer than the approximately 7,200 U.S. TNW now deployed on the continent—a force believed by many to be dangerously excessive. The second alternative calls for a reduction in both the size of the deployment and the vulnerability to preemption or capture of the remaining systems, with the goal of a U.S. tactical nuclear deployment in Europe that is neither superabundant nor a temptation to surprise attack. The third alternative involves a major restructuring of the deployment coupled with a radical reorientation of tactical nuclear doctrine. The present relatively high yield TNW would be largely replaced by less destructive, miniaturized devices designed primarily for battlefield use; these "mini-nukes" would represent a substitute for rather than a supplement to conventional defense, thus requiring profound changes in current NATO strategy. The fourth alternative envisages the renunciation of a U.S. tactical nuclear defense of Europe and the removal of all U.S. TNW from the continent.

The author recognizes that many of the issues and proposals addressed here are not new; however, he is convinced that most will remain highly relevant to the future course of U.S. tactical nuclear policy in NATO. Since tactical nuclear war has never been a reality, any study of the subject is compelled to rely upon highly speculative literature. A further constraint is the official secrecy that veils much information on U.S. TNW, especially the costs associated with the European deployment; accurate data on Soviet weapons have, of course, been even harder to obtain.

CHAPTER TWO

TACTICAL NUCLEAR WEAPONS:
DEFINITIONS AND CATEGORIES

A major problem in any discussion of TNW is the lack of a precise definition of the term itself. This is reflected in the following exchange between Senator Stuart Symington and Army Chief of Staff Creighton Abrams:

> Senator SYMINGTON. . . . today weapons considered tactical are so infinitely more lethal than the Hiroshima bomb. One wonders . . . what is going to be destroyed rather than the weapon per se. The difference between strategic and tactical is getting hard to distinguish. If one fighter plane, very short range, reached Japan from Iwo Jima and knocked out a Japanese plant, it was performing a strategic mission. As you know, in the Battle of the Bulge, we used our largest bombers in tactical fashion. In any case I think we must get our ducks in a row as to whether we would use tactical nuclear weapons without running a serious danger of getting into an all-out war. . . .
>
> So what is a tactical weapon and what is a strategic weapon? I am interested in your thoughts on that and this subject in general.
>
> General ABRAMS. Senator, first of all, I think both of us know that *no one can say today* . . . with all that we know, and all that we think we know . . . [emphasis added].[1]

Definitions of tactical nuclear weapons and warfare are plentiful and disparate. Few, however, are precise and none is completely satisfactory. One analyst has defined TNW simply as "nuclear weapons designed to support land forces,"[2] while another believes them to be those weapons "designed to influence the land or air defense battle *directly,* rather than indirectly (for example, by interdicting an enemy's lines of communication or by carrying a threat to his homeland)."[3] Tactical nuclear war-

---

1. *Fiscal Year 1974 Authorization,* Hearings before the Senate Committee on Armed Services, 93 Cong. 1 sess. (1973), pt. 2, p. 566.
2. Morton H. Halperin, *Defense Strategies for the Seventies* (Little, Brown, 1971), p. 5.
3. John Newhouse and others, *U.S. Troops in Europe: Issues, Costs, and Choices* (Brookings Institution, 1971), p. 45.

fare has been defined as "the use of nuclear weapons for limited tactical military purposes,"[4] although officially it is designated as "a conflict between the land forces and associated air and naval forces of two or more nations in which nuclear weapons are limited to the defeat of opposing forces in a theater of operations. Implicit in this definition is the condition that a strategic nuclear exchange on the belligerents' homelands does not occur."[5] Much of the literature makes no meaningful distinction (if, indeed, there is one) between tactical nuclear weapons and the tactical *uses* of nuclear weapons and proposes no analytically useful boundary between TNW and strategic weapons. Often ignored is the fact that a weapon that might be tactical for one country would be inevitably strategic for another. Use of TNW by the United States on West German soil, for example, even though it did not provoke a strategic exchange between the United States and the USSR, would nevertheless be of strategic significance to the Germans.

There are two basic approaches to defining TNW. The first and less satisfactory is based on yield. The destructive power of nuclear weapons is calculated in equivalent weights of the conventional high explosive TNT. Yields of U.S. TNW currently range from several hundred tons of TNT to over one million tons (or megaton). Some analysts have suggested that all warheads below one megaton be considered tactical, with more powerful weapons designated as strategic; others believe the boundary should be set much lower—at the 500-kiloton, 100-kiloton, or even the sub-kiloton level. Implicit in this classification is an attempt to define as tactical those weapons that promise to generate the least amount of collateral damage commensurate with the destruction of military targets. This attempt is complicated by the fact that the magnitude of collateral damage varies widely according to terrain, weather, altitude of detonation, proximity of civilian population, and a host of other factors. And, in fact, many U.S. weapons designated as tactical possess yields far too large to permit any meaningful discrimination between civilian and military targets in highly industrialized and heavily populated Central Europe. The *Pershing* missiles presently deployed on the continent, for example, carry warheads that render the Hiroshima bomb tiny by comparison and in some cases surpass the destructiveness

4. Robert M. Lawrence, "On Tactical Nuclear War: Part I," *Revue Militaire Générale* (January 1971), p. 46.

5. Department of the Army, Field Manual 100-30 (Test), *Tactical Nuclear Operations* (Headquarters, Department of the Army, August 1971), p. 2–1.

of those mounted on such strategic weapons as the *Minuteman III, Polaris A3,* and *Poseidon.*[6] This overlap of yields further blurs a distinction between TNW and strategic arms based on destructive potential.

The primary difficulty with the yield approach, however, is that it ignores the differing ranges of various delivery systems. Even the smallest warhead, if delivered on a target understood by both sides to be strategic, could no longer be considered a tactical weapon; in the context of present NATO strategy, this means any target located inside the Soviet Union, since even a limited nuclear strike on Soviet territory would almost certainly provoke a strategic riposte by the USSR. Conversely, strategic weapons can and have been employed in a tactical mode. A recent addition to the example cited by Senator Symington is U.S. use of B-52s against battlefield targets in Indochina.

Although no currently deployed ground-launched U.S. TNW possesses the range to reach the Soviet Union,[7] the same cannot be said of many nuclear-capable tactical aircraft. These would include the three squadrons of F-111s based in England and the more than 500 nuclear-capable F-4s deployed on the continent. Although oriented toward tactical missions, both types of aircraft are capable of delivering bombs ranging from 0.1 kiloton to over one megaton on targets inside European Russia. The potential strategic role of these and other nuclear forward-based systems (FBS) has been the topic of debate in recent East-West negotiations and is of particular concern to the Soviet Union, which sought unsuccessfully to have FBS placed on the agenda of SALT I and is pressing for their inclusion in the current MBFR negotiations.

It is this classification of nuclear weapons according to range of delivery system that constitutes the second basic approach to defining TNW. Under it, TNW are considered all weapons that are employable in a theater of operations (for example, non-Soviet Europe) but could not or would not be used against the United States or the Soviet Union. This definition automatically encompasses all U.S. and Soviet ground-launched TNW as well as weapons carried by aircraft that, from present locations and without the benefit of in-flight refueling, are incapable of

---

6. The yield of the Hiroshima bomb was approximately 13 kilotons, while warheads of the *Pershing* missile range from 60 to 400 kilotons. The multiple independently targeted reentry vehicles (MIRV) of the *Minuteman 3, Polaris A3,* and *Poseidon* represent yields of 200, 200, and 50 kilotons, respectively.

7. With the exception of *Pershing* missiles launched from certain West German border areas.

reaching and returning from each other's homelands.[8] Controversy continues, of course, over the proper delineation of systems designated tactical but possessing "strategic" ranges, such as the F-111 and F-4. While the United States prefers to treat these systems as tactical, the Soviet Union continues to stress their strategic capabilities.

There is, at least theoretically, no limitation on yields under the range approach, since geography rather than warhead size is the determining factor. Nevertheless, it is difficult to envisage the theater use of devices in the multimegaton range. The employment in Central Europe of such weapons as the U.S. *Titan II* (5 to 10 megatons) or the Soviet SS-9 SCARP[9] (20 to 25 megatons) missiles, for example, would serve no tactical purpose because the magnitude of destruction would negate any conceivable military or territorial gain to the user. Similarly, it is hard to imagine the use of very low yield weapons (2 kilotons or below) against strategic targets. The limited range of many systems would, or course, prohibit such use. Moreover, the requirement for greater destruction over a wider area that is generally associated with strategic targets could not be met by small yields.

It is thus clear that the term tactical nuclear weapon is very ambiguous. Much more satisfying is the concept of tactical versus strategic *use* of nuclear weapons, which focuses on the types of designated targets rather than inherent capabilities of the weapon systems themselves. Target nature as the determinant for what are tactical and what are strategic nuclear weapons not only is implicit in the official Department of Defense definition of tactical nuclear warfare[10] but also formed the basis for deciding which weapon systems, with the exception of strategic bombers and nuclear cruise missiles (which were excluded for other reasons), would not be discussed at SALT I.

In this study, therefore, tactical nuclear weapons are defined as all nuclear weapon systems other than strategic bombers (and the bombs they carry), nuclear cruise missiles, and land- and sea-based intercontinental ballistic missiles. Although, conceivably, any of these strategic

8. Nuclear-capable aircraft that can make only one-way trips to strategic targets are usually not counted as part of the strategic threat, although they are expected to become a topic of discussion in future SALT negotiations.

9. For ease of identification, unless otherwise specified, Soviet weapon systems are capitalized and U.S. and West European systems italicized throughout this monograph.

10. In addition to the definition of tactical nuclear war cited above in the U.S. Army Field Manual, the *Annual Defense Department Report: FY 1974* states (p. 27) that "theater nuclear conflict involves the use of nuclear weapons against or by U.S. or allied forces overseas, but not against the United States itself."

weapons could be employed for tactical purposes, both their design and the doctrines governing their use make such usage unlikely. A possible exception would be the several U.S. and British *Polaris* submarines assigned to the Supreme Allied Commander Europe (SACEUR). This definition permits the separation of U.S. TNW into three categories.

1. *Battlefield* or *short-range theater nuclear weapons* are weapons designed to influence *directly* the outcome of combat by destroying engaged enemy military forces. Generally of low yield (0.1 to 2 kilotons) and limited range (up to approximately 70 nautical miles), they include all artillery-delivered nuclear projectiles, the *Lance* and *Honest John* missiles, and various types of bombs.

2. *Long-range theater nuclear weapons* are weapons designed to influence *indirectly* the outcome of combat by interdicting the movement of enemy troops and supplies to and from the battle area or by destroying rear area installations—airfields, marshaling yards, supply depots—vital to the enemy's continued prosecution of hostilities. Although some battlefield nuclear weapons could be employed for these purposes, theater weapons generally possess higher yields (3 to 400 kilotons) and longer ranges (up to 400 miles). They include the *Pershing* and perhaps the *Sergeant* missiles as well as a number of bombs.

3. *Semistrategic nuclear weapons* encompass all nuclear weapons that are designated by the United States for theater use but that could nevertheless reach and return from targets inside the Soviet Union from present locations. Prominent among these systems are the F-111 and forward-deployed F-4 fighter bombers.

In addition to these weapons, all of which possess an offensive (counterattack) warfighting capability, the United States maintains in the European area large numbers of sea-based TNW and surface-to-air *Nike-Hercules* missiles, as well as an unknown number of atomic demolition munitions (ADM). Most of these systems, however, are purely defensive in orientation and will be discussed in subsequent chapters.

CHAPTER THREE

RATIONALES PAST AND PRESENT

Two basic rationales underlie U.S. deployment of TNW in the European area. First, despite mounting evidence to the contrary, TNW continue to be viewed by some as the only economically and politically feasible means of offsetting what is still perceived by many Western observers as an overwhelming communist superiority in conventional military forces on the continent. The presence of TNW, it is said, not only enhances deterrence of major conventional aggression and Soviet first use of nuclear weapons, but also permits NATO to maintain smaller conventional forces. Second, TNW are believed to augment the credibility of U.S. willingness to employ its strategic deterrent on behalf of Europe because their designated use in the event of a collapse of conventional arms would constitute an intermediate and postnuclear threshold "link" to that deterrent. Neither of these two arguments has gone unchallenged; indeed, they continue to generate strong debate.

The first attempts to investigate the potential function of nuclear weapons in ground warfare were undertaken by a group of scientists during a series of conferences known as Project Vista held at the California Institute of Technology in 1948. The following year, Chairman of the Joint Chiefs of Staff General Omar Bradley proposed that the United States develop and acquire TNW to offset Soviet conventional superiority in Europe. In 1951, the United States began testing nuclear devices of one-kiloton yield and below (weapons previously tested in the postwar era having ranged from 18 to 49 kilotons), although it was not until October 1953 that President Eisenhower authorized the Joint Chiefs of Staff to base their plans on employing tactical and strategic nuclear weapons to counter conventional attack whenever it was deemed militarily advantageous to do so.

In that same month began the deployment of U.S. TNW in the European area, starting with the first of a number of 85-ton, 280-mm atomic "cannon," followed in 1954 by the *Regulus* and *Honest John* missiles. For the next three years, U.S. weapons were the only TNW stationed in Europe; although the USSR decided to acquire TNW in 1954, the first weapons were not introduced into Soviet ground forces until 1957. The Truman and Eisenhower administrations concluded that severe budgetary constraints, reinforced by public support for reduced defense spending, prohibited NATO's mustering a nonnuclear deterrent sufficient to balance an enormous Soviet superiority in conventional forces backed by a rapacious foreign policy. That budgetary considerations were paramount in the early 1950s was underlined by the then Air Force Chief of Staff General Nathan Twining in testimony before the Senate Armed Services Committee: "a new strategy built around the use of atomic weapons" was necessary to permit the United States "to reduce our forces considerably" and the "only way we can provide the forces for the country within a reasonable standard of financing."[1]

The decision to rely on nuclear weapons rather than the more costly conventional forces for national defense—epitomized by the adoption in 1954 of the massive retaliation strategy—was also stimulated in no small part by the bitter and frustrating experience of U.S. conventional arms in Korea and by the failure of Western European allies to meet the conventional force goal of 96 divisions agreed upon at the Lisbon Conference in 1952. It was, moreover, in keeping with the long-standing U.S. tradition of trading technology for manpower.

The belief that TNW could redress the conventional force imbalance in Europe and thus permit relatively small investment in nonnuclear forces is still offered as a rationale for the deployment of U.S. TNW on the continent, despite what many consider to be its invalidation by subsequent developments. Reliance on a nuclear defense in which conventional forces would serve primarily as a "tripwire" to establish the fact of aggression and to "justify" a nuclear response appeared warranted at a time when the Soviet Union possessed neither TNW nor a credible strategic deterrent. By the early 1960s, however, the USSR had equipped its ground forces with TNW and was striving hard to establish a credible second-strike capability in the strategic realm; these two developments terminated the likelihood that a NATO first use of TNW would not be countered in kind. Indeed, as is shown in Chapter 5, both Soviet military

1. Quoted in Robert Endicott Osgood, *NATO: The Entangling Alliance* (University of Chicago Press, 1962), p. 122.

doctrine and wargames conducted by the Warsaw Pact continue strongly to imply that Pact forces would employ TNW from the very start of hostilities—if for no other reason than to preempt a NATO first use.

The implications for NATO of a two-sided tactical nuclear war emerged slowly and some are still the subject of contention. One conclusion, however, was obvious early on: a conflict characterized by the use of TNW by adversaries possessing large numbers of such weapons would be far more destructive to Western Europe than a war distinguished by unilateral NATO use, particularly in light of continued Soviet reliance on TNW of substantially greater yields and lingering radiological effects. This conclusion was strengthened by the presumption of the Pact as the attacker, which suggested that many if not most devices inevitably would be detonated in Germany and other densely populated countries of Western Europe. As the English physicist P. M. S. Blackett pointed out in 1962, even a "limited" tactical nuclear war in Europe would be a strategic one for Europeans. He went on to surmise that, because the USSR also possessed TNW, "the initiation by the West of tactical nuclear war might either hasten military defeat, or lead to the destruction of Europe . . . or both."[2] Three years earlier, Bernard Brodie had concluded that the "moment we start visualizing [TNW] as being used reciprocally, their use ceases to look overwhelmingly advantageous to us," and that, in any event, a "people saved by us through our free use of nuclear weapons over their territories would probably be the last that would ever ask us to help them."[3]

These judgments appeared already to have been confirmed in two tactical nuclear wargames conducted in 1955. Although both exercises entailed only unilateral and, by contemporary standards, limited employment of TNW on the part of NATO, their results strongly indicated that reliance on tactical nuclear defense would lead to devastation of the very Western Europe that NATO is designed to protect. In Operation Sage Brush, conducted in Louisiana, 275 TNW of from 2 to 40 kilotons were "detonated" in a limited military operation. The assessors "reported that the destruction was so great that no such thing as limited or purely tactical nuclear war was possible in such an area."[4] A second exercise, Carte Blanche, was undertaken in Western Europe. In the space of forty-eight hours a total of 335 devices were "exploded," 268

2. P. M. S. Blackett, *Studies of War* (London: Oliver and Boyd, 1962), p. 63.
3. Bernard Brodie, *Strategy in the Missile Age* (Princeton University Press, 1959), pp. 321, 324–25.
4. Blackett, *Studies of War,* p. 63.

of them on German territory. German casualties, not including those attributable to residual radiation, were estimated at between 1.5 and 1.7 million dead and 3.5 million wounded. These figures compare with total German civilian casualties inflicted by Allied bombing throughout the entire Second World War of 305,000 killed and 780,000 wounded. The impact of Carte Blanche on German public opinion was predictable and stemmed from the realization that the use of TNW "will not defend Europe, but destroy it."[5]

Further wargames and studies undertaken by the Defense Department in the 1960s continued to reaffirm these conclusions:

> Even under the most favorable assumptions, it appeared that between 2 and 20 million Europeans would be killed, with widespread damage to the economy of the affected area and a high risk of 100 million dead if the war escalated to attacks on cities. In the light of this, it was difficult to see how initiating a tactical nuclear war would satisfy the United States' basic goal of defending the people and territories of NATO Europe. When the defense of Europe is seen to entail its nuclear destruction, the European incentive to permit the use of nuclear weapons on its soil diminishes rapidly.[6]

The implications of two-sided tactical nuclear war for conventional forces were less obvious. Although most observers concluded that a nuclear environment—or the threat of one—would compel the dispersion of ground and tactical air forces in order to deny the enemy lucrative targets for nuclear strikes, they disagreed as to whether this meant that fewer or more forces were required.[7] Many continued to believe

---

5. Helmut Schmidt, *Defense or Retaliation* (Praeger, 1962), p. 101.

6. Alain C. Enthoven and K. Wayne Smith, *How Much Is Enough? Shaping the Defense Program 1961–1969* (Harper and Row, 1971), p. 128.

7. For a comprehensive analysis of the implications of tactical nuclear warfare for conventional force structure and tactical deployment patterns, see Otto Heilbrunn, *Conventional Warfare in the Nuclear Age* (Praeger, 1965). For Heilbrunn, the key to the survivability of conventional forces in a nuclear environment is the avoidance of concentration except when in close contact with the enemy, in which case both sides would be reluctant to use TNW for fear of destroying their own forces. Dispersion also places a premium on increasing the mobility of deployed formations, since the greater distances separating them serve to constrain their ability to provide mutual support. These principles represent the foundation of present U.S. and Soviet doctrine. In Department of the Army, Field Manual FM 100-30 (Test), *Tactical Nuclear Operations* (Headquarters, Department of the Army, August 1971), it is stated that in a nuclear environment "tactical operations are characterized by great dispersion both laterally and in depth; redundance, especially of command and control headquarters; and the employment of small, highly mobile tactical elements." A division, for example, is expected to cover a front of 36–50 kilometers and a depth of 60–80 kilometers; in a nonnuclear environment, the operational area of a division has for planning purposes been defined as not exceeding a front of 18–24 kilometers and a depth of equal distance.

that the development of TNW was the key to low-cost defense, based on the assumption that conventional forces could easily be traded for deployment of TNW. This line of reasoning was reflected in a speech delivered in 1954 by General Alfred M. Gruenther, Supreme Allied Commander in Europe: "If seventy divisions, for example, are needed to establish a conventional line of defense between the Alps and the Baltic, then seventy minus X divisions equipped with atomic weapons would be needed."[8]

A growing body of opinion, however, was reaching a contrary conclusion: namely, that a two-sided tactical nuclear war would require more rather than fewer conventional forces. The logic behind this assessment, which continues to dominate within the U.S. military, is compelling. The very character of a tactical nuclear war, it is argued, would not only dictate a much larger battlefield (and thus negate the potential economies of dispersion) but also generate substantially higher rates of attrition. These implications were discerned as early as 1956 by General Matthew B. Ridgway:

There are a number of sound and logical reasons why a field army of the atomic age may have to be bigger than its predecessors of the past. The complex new weapons themselves—the atomic cannon, rockets, and guided missiles—require far more men to serve and maintain them than did the simpler field pieces of World War II and Korea. The prospect of sudden and enormous casualties, inflicted by the enemy with his own new weapons, makes necessary the training of replacements in great numbers for the dead, and a medical establishment larger than ever to care for the sick and wounded. In the main, though, the changing shape of the battlefield itself sets the requirements for more men. The battle zones of World War II within which actual ground combat took place were rarely as much as twenty-five miles in depth. Penetrations of armored and airborne forces in the battle areas of the future may well extend two hundred miles or even more in depth, and only by great dispersion, in the wars of the future, will ground elements be able to survive.[9]

Ridgway's contention that the security, handling, and maintenance of TNW would require substantial manpower that might otherwise be employed in a conventional role seems justified. For example, of the 199,000-man U.S. Army Europe (USAREUR), 23,000, or about 12 percent, are presently assigned to the Missile Forces, which constitute USAREUR's primary repository of surface-to-surface tactical nuclear missile capabilities. Thousands of other troops are assigned to units

8. Osgood, *NATO,* p. 109.
9. Matthew B. Ridgway, *Soldier: The Memoirs of Matthew B. Ridgway* (Harper, 1956), pp. 296–97.

charged with the protection and maintenance of nuclear warheads, bombs, and their storage sites.

The idea, once prevalent among Western defense analysts, that large conventional forces were not required because small ground forces equipped with tactical nuclear weapons could contain a strong conventional attack by the East was based on the assumption that the opponent would have to concentrate for the attack and thus offer a good nuclear target. This concept became outmoded when the East also equipped its forces with tactical nuclear weapons. The attacker, it is true, may no longer be able to concentrate large forces for an offensive—unless he takes a calculated risk—but large concentrations are not necessarily required any more for an attack, since the defense can no longer mass forces without risk either. If the defense is not concentrated, the attacker can more easily infiltrate and reach the comparative safety of the defender's rear which the latter is unlikely to subject to nuclear bombardment because he would cut off his own supply lines and retreat routes. There is also still some scope, to say the least, for operations of the attacker in the rear of the defense; they make it possible to thin out the attacker's front even more.

It has also been said that the defense, by laying waste large areas with atomic bursts, could always force the attacker to concentrate at selected places and thus gain a decisive advantage. But this argument is no longer valid either since the attacker can now do likewise.

If fewer troops are required at any given time to man the defenses, more are needed over a period to replace the greater number of casualties expected in a nuclear war. Furthermore, one must not lose sight of the fact that the war will possibly be fought on NATO soil, and the NATO defense will be more reluctant than the attacker to squander nuclear devices. What the individual strikes of the attacker may lack in effectiveness, he can easily make up by the number of strikes. If there is an advantage in a tactical nuclear exchange on NATO soil it is unlikely to be with the West. It seems bound, in fact, to suffer more.[10]

It was perhaps partly the increasingly doubtful validity of these rationales for the development and deployment of TNW that prompted the Kennedy administration to put forward a new justification for them— that TNW served to enhance the credibility of the U.S. strategic deterrent by providing a link between the possible failure of conventional defense in Europe and U.S. willingness to employ its ultimate weapons. It is important to remember that until the last years of the Eisenhower administration the use of TNW "was not visualized apart from strategic nuclear war"; under the doctrine of massive retaliation, which called for the immediate employment of the U.S. strategic deterrent in response to

10. Heilbrunn, *Conventional Warfare,* pp. 19–20.

any form of major Soviet aggression, TNW were to be "used in a mopup action after a strategic exchange."[11]

Under the strategy of flexible response, however, conventional defense was for the first time established as the preferred riposte to aggression in Europe and elsewhere. Nuclear weapons, although still the option of last resort, were envisaged as a hedge against the possible collapse of conventional defense rather than NATO's first and only response to attack. The role of TNW was deemed little more than a psychological reinforcement of the credibility of U.S. willingness to employ its strategic deterrent in defense of its European allies, for President Kennedy firmly believed that "inevitably, the use of small nuclear armaments will lead to larger and larger nuclear armaments on both sides, until the world-wide holocaust has begun."[12]

Both the Kennedy and Johnson administrations held that even small TNW were "extremely destructive devices and hardly the preferred weapons to defend such heavily populated areas as Europe" and, further, that they could not meaningfully be substituted for conventional forces.[13] Both also subscribed heartily to the so-called firebreak theory that held that the wartime detonation of any nuclear device would lead to a strategic exchange, and, therefore, that the real watershed in escalation lay not between the use of TNW and strategic weapons but rather between conventional warfare and nuclear warfare. The conditions under which TNW might be employed were thus restricted to situations in which "the opponent employs such weapons first, or any attack by conventional forces which puts Europe in danger of being overrun."[14] These two threats continue to constitute the foundation of the perceived *deterrent* value of U.S. TNW in Europe, although the credibility attaching itself to the actual use of at least the present deployment is seriously questioned even by those who wish to revert to a predominantly nuclear defense of the continent.

Nevertheless, the significance of TNW even as a link to the strategic deterrent has appreciably diminished in an era of secure U.S. and Soviet strategic retaliatory capabilities. To Europeans and to many Americans,

11. Denis M. Gormley, "NATO's Tactical Nuclear Option: Past, Present and Future," *Military Review,* vol. 53 (September 1973), p. 5.

12. John F. Kennedy, *The Strategy of Peace* (Harper, 1960), p. 185.

13. Testimony of Secretary of Defense Robert S. McNamara, *Department of Defense Appropriations for 1964,* Hearings before a Subcommittee of the Committee on Appropriations, 88 Cong. 1 sess. (1963), pt. 1, p. 102.

14. Ibid.

parity has served to reduce the credibility of the strategic deterrent and, by extension, of ideas that the use of TNW might pave the way for its employment. The logic underlying this conclusion appears unassailable unless one assumes a disposition on the part of the United States to provoke its own possible destruction under circumstances other than direct attack upon its own territory. It was DeGaulle's rejection of precisely this assumption that led to France's withdrawal from NATO's integrated military commands and its decision to build a *force de frappe* free of foreign constraints. The waning credibility of a U.S. strategic nuclear response to an invasion of Europe has in fact been officially admitted, if somewhat belatedly, by the United States:

In the late 1960s the effectiveness of American strategic nuclear forces was measured by a criterion known as "assured destruction." This concept assumed that deterrence could be maintained if it were clear that following a large-scale nuclear strike the United States could retaliate and inflict an unacceptable level of damage on the population and industry of the attacker.

In the 1970s strategic doctrine must meet different criteria. While the specter of an unacceptable response is fundamental to deterrence, the ability to kill tens of millions of people is not the only or necessarily the most effective deterrent to every challenge. Such a drastic course can be credibly reserved only for the most overwhelming threats to national survival . . .

A different strategic doctrine is required in this decade when potential adversaries possess large and more flexible nuclear forces. The threat of an all-out nuclear response . . . might not be as credible a deterrent as it was in the 1960s. An aggressor, in the unlikely event of nuclear war, might choose to employ nuclear weapons selectively and in limited numbers for limited objectives. No President should ever be in the position where his only option in meeting such aggression is an all-out nuclear response.[15]

Another development that has cast doubt upon the significance of TNW in the overall military balance is the growing conviction, at least in the United States, that Europe can be defended without resort to nuclear weapons. Presumption of the continent's conventional indefensibility is of course the sine qua non of most arguments for nuclear defense and as such deserves investigation. The postwar image of a militarily naked Western Europe at the mercy of hundreds of Soviet divisions poised along the Central Front continues to linger in the public mind, and proponents of nuclear defense remain convinced that "the West cannot field the quantitative and qualitative conventional capabilities necessary to halt, let alone defeat, a . . . conventional attack . . .

15. *U.S. Foreign Policy for the 1970's:* A Report to the Congress by Richard M. Nixon, President of the United States (May 3, 1973), pp. 183–84.

by the Warsaw Pact."[16] The validity of this judgment cannot, of course, be tested conclusively in peacetime; but the very real possibility of conventional defeat has always existed and its implications should continue to be a prominent concern of strategic planners.

However, several contemporary analyses provide grounds for much greater optimism than in the past. Enthoven and Smith, by forswearing traditional but meaningless division counts and concentrating on the more important structural and qualitative indicators of military capabilities, concluded in 1971 that Europe could be defended not only without resort to nuclear arms but also within the framework of existing conventional forces at the disposal of NATO.[17] A similar appraisal is contained in the *Annual Defense Department Report, FY 1975,* which projects fifty-eight Pact divisions as the "immediate" threat and eighty to ninety divisions as the "mobilized threat" to Western Europe.[18] These numbers, although impressive on paper, are decidedly less so in reality because Soviet and Eastern European divisions possess substantially less firepower and but little more than one-half the manpower fielded by opposing U.S. and allied divisions.

A third assessment, by Richard D. Lawrence and Jeffrey Record, posited the NATO–Warsaw Pact conventional force ratios in the crucial Central Region shown below in Table 3-1. It is apparent that the present (M-day) balance of forces in the Center is generally not unfavorable to NATO (including France), given the widely held presumption that the Pact, as the attacker, would need to muster a minimum superiority over NATO of two to one—and many believe three to one—in all of the above categories if it is to have a reasonable chance of successfully invading and occupying Western Europe. With few variations the same holds true following thirty and even sixty days of simultaneous or nearly

---

16. Philip A. Karber, "Nuclear Weapons and 'Flexible Response,'" *Orbis,* vol. 14 (Summer 1970), p. 288. Other proponents of nuclear defense who share similar views include Robert M. Lawrence, "On Tactical Nuclear War," *Revue Militaire Générale* (January 1971); James H. Polk, "The Realities of Tactical Nuclear Defense," *Orbis,* vol. 17 (Summer 1973); Stephen T. Possony, "NATO's Defense Posture," *Ordnance,* vol. 14 (July–August 1969); R. C. Richardson, "Can NATO Fashion a New Strategy?" *Orbis,* vol. 17 (Summer 1973); Andre Beaufré, "Security and Defense in Western Europe," *Orbis,* vol. 13 (Spring 1969); Samuel T. Cohen, "Tactical Nuclear War and U.S. Military Strategy," *Orbis,* vol. 15 (Spring 1971); and Wynfred Joshua, "A Strategic Concept for the Defense of Europe," *Orbis,* vol. 17 (Summer 1973).

17. *How Much Is Enough?*

18. Secretary of Defense James R. Schlesinger, *Annual Defense Department Report, FY 1975* (1974), pp. 87–89.

Table 3-1. Warsaw Pact and NATO Forces Available for Combat in the Central Region on M Day, M + 30, and M + 60
Thousands

Force component	M day	M + 30	M + 60
Total deployed military manpower			
Total Warsaw Pact	576	1,076	1,241
USSR	339	677	842
Total NATO	660	1,045	1,105
U.S.	200	285	345
Ground combat troops			
Total Warsaw Pact	432	807	931
USSR	254	502	632
Total NATO	365	555	585
U.S.	90	130	160
Tanks			
Total Warsaw Pact	11.8	20.3	21.8
USSR	6.9	12.9	15.2
Total NATO	6.7	7.7	8.2
U.S.	1.2	1.9	2.3
Tactical combat aircraft			
Total Warsaw Pact	5.5	6.7	8.4
USSR	3.7	4.9	6.6
Total NATO	2.7	4.2	4.7
U.S.	0.6	2.0	2.5

Source: Richard D. Lawrence and Jeffrey Record, *U.S. Force Structure in NATO: An Alternative* (Brookings Institution, 1974), p. 46.

simultaneous mobilization, unless a number of highly questionable assumptions are made about the USSR's willingness to strip its Far Eastern defenses, the combat readiness of most Russian divisions, and the degree of East European support the Soviets could count on for an offensive against Western Europe. Only in tanks does the Pact have an overwhelming numerical superiority, and even this margin is somewhat offset by the notably higher quality of tactical aircraft and armor at the disposal of the Atlantic Alliance as well as NATO's heavy investment in modern antitank defenses, whose effectiveness was so spectacularly demonstrated by both sides during the Mideast War of 1973.

Thus, the weaknesses of NATO's conventional defense posture do not appear attributable to an insufficiency of forces but rather to the way in which those forces are organized and disposed. Nevertheless, given the assumption of the Pact as the aggressor and the high probability of substantial "political" warning time before a major invasion,[19]

19. The expectation of warning time, which would permit NATO to supplement its forces already forward deployed on the continent and to prepare the battle area, is a reasonable one; Pact forces now available for an attack, unless

a successful conventional defense of Europe seems not only feasible but also well within the grasp of the forces now deployed on the continent.

In sum, the basic rationales underlying the U.S. deployment of TNW in the European area seem far less persuasive than they were in the 1950s and early 1960s. The view that TNW can offset Pact superiority in conventional forces—a superiority which itself is increasingly less apparent to many observers—may have been fully justified at a time when the West alone possessed such weapons. It is of questionable validity, however, in a military environment that promises mutual use of TNW; the resulting destruction could threaten the survival not only of the countries that are the object of NATO's protection but also of their armed forces, whose ability to maintain a coherent defense on a nuclear battlefield would be contingent on a capacity to replace massive losses of both personnel and equipment. Similarly, the value of TNW as a link to the strategic deterrent is doubtful in an era that has witnessed the dwindling credibility of that deterrent.

On the other hand, the mere presence of U.S. TNW on the continent, even if not supported by a believable warfighting doctrine, probably does impose upon Soviet military planners a significant element of tactical uncertainty. This uncertainty may enhance deterrence of conventional aggression. However, it is perhaps equally likely that in an acute crisis it would serve to reduce the prospect of nonnuclear conflict by encouraging a preemptive Pact nuclear strike.

---

substantially augmented from the USSR by reinforcements whose transfer to the front could not escape detection, would have little chance of successfully carrying NATO Center.

CHAPTER FOUR

PRESENT U.S. TACTICAL NUCLEAR POSTURE IN NATO

U.S. tactical nuclear posture in Europe is defined not only by the number and capabilities of the weapons themselves, but also by the command and control arrangements and the doctrine that regulate their deployment and use.

U.S. Capabilities

The United States maintains about 7,000 tactical nuclear warheads in the European area,[1] approximately two-thirds of which are intended for allied use. Deployed delivery systems encompass nuclear-capable artillery, surface-to-surface missiles, surface-to-air missiles, and a variety of tactical aircraft. Atomic demolition munitions (ADM) are also present on the continent.

Most of these delivery systems are dual-capable—that is, capable of using either conventional or nuclear ordnance. How many of them would be employed in a nuclear role in the event of hostilities is, of course, unknown. Current NATO strategic guidance envisages at least an initial conventional defense against nonnuclear aggression. Even were the conflict to become nuclear it is probable that most systems would continue to be used in a conventional mode, particularly in tactical situations where the proximity of friendly forces precluded the use of nuclear weapons. Some tactical aircraft and missile systems, however, are currently designated solely for nuclear employment and are maintained on Quick Reaction Alert (QRA). Nuclear-loaded and ready for instant launching, QRA weapons include some U.S. Air Force F-4s

1. The exact number is classified. Former Secretary of Defense Robert S. McNamara stated in 1967 that there were then about 7,000 TNW in the European area; the following year his successor, Clark M. Clifford, put the figure at 7,200.

19

and F-111s, some *Pershing* missiles, and a number of West European planes.

The range (and, for aircraft, the operational radius) of U.S. TNW varies from eight nautical miles[2] for the 155-mm howitzer to about 1,500 miles for the F-111. Warhead yields extend from approximately 0.1 kiloton, deliverable by both artillery and aircraft, to over one megaton deliverable only by aircraft. A prominent feature of U.S. warheads is selectivity of yield. Most warheads are configured to permit a choice of at least two yields, one high, one low, simply by "dialing" the preferred alternative before employment. Selectivity not only enhances tactical flexibility but also permits greater latitude in attempts to minimize collateral damage.

Another notable aspect of U.S. TNW in Europe is the age of most delivery systems. With the exception of the *Lance* missile, which is now replacing the *Honest John* and *Sergeant,* all U.S. ground-launched systems are at least ten years old. The same is true of the designs of most U.S. tactical aircraft.

Ground-Launched Systems

Ground-launched TNW deployed with U.S. forces in Europe fall into three categories: artillery, missiles, and ADM. The characteristics of each system are shown in Table 4-1.

ARTILLERY. Deployed nuclear-capable artillery consists of several hundred M-109 155-mm and M-110 8-inch howitzers. Both of these systems are self-propelled, dual-capable, and intended for battlefield use only. Projectile yields range from as low as 100 tons to several kilotons.

MISSILES. U.S. tactical nuclear surface-to-surface missiles (SSM) in Europe number about 200 and include the *Honest John, Sergeant, Pershing,* and *Lance.* Range estimates in Table 4-1 show that only the *Pershing* may be classified exclusively as a long-range theater nuclear weapon (it is also the only SSM maintained on QRA), the best being

2. Distances here and throughout the book, unless otherwise specified, are calculated in nautical miles (1 nautical mile = 1.14 statute miles or 1.92 kilometers).

suited principally for battlefield employment. Neither the *Pershing* nor the *Lance* are dual-capable, although the U.S. Army is actively pursuing an engineering development program for a nonnuclear warhead for the *Lance*. All four SSM are mounted on self-propelled carriers, although only the *Lance* has good cross-country mobility since it is the only missile mounted on a tracked vehicle. The *Pershing*, moreover, must be dismounted prior to launching. Launch preparation time ranges from less than an hour for the *Lance* to about two hours for the *Pershing*. Warhead yields vary from about one kiloton to as much as 400 kilotons.

U.S. forces also possess about 150 *Nike-Hercules* surface-to-air missiles (SAM). Designed for air defense, the *Nike-Hercules* can be employed in a surface-to-surface mode, although its limited range (up to twenty miles) and relative inaccuracy against ground targets render it notably inferior as an SSM to the *Lance* or even the *Honest John*.

ATOMIC DEMOLITION MUNITIONS. Little is publicly known about atomic demolition munitions. Essentially nuclear land mines designed to block or canalize invading forces by triggering landslides or cratering corridors of invasion, they are purely defensive devices and must be placed underground before detonation. It is generally believed, however, that no ADM are presently prechambered in NATO Europe, with the possible exception of Turkey. Although an unknown number of ADM are stored on the continent, European governments (notably West Germany) so far have refused for political reasons to permit their emplacement.[3]

Tactical Air Systems

European-deployed tactical aircraft of U.S. forces configured for delivery of nuclear ordnance include about 500 Air Force F-4s (over half of which are based in West Germany) and 70 F-111s (all of which

---

3. According to a recent report, "no chambers have been specifically constructed in Europe for ADM's, although there are chambers for conventional explosives. These chambers are not considered to be as satisfactory as chambers prepared specifically for ADM's, some because they are shallower and would result in greater fallout." *U.S. Security Issues in Europe: Burden Sharing and Offset, MBFR and Nuclear Weapons,* a staff report prepared for the Subcommittee on U.S. Security Agreements and Commitments Abroad of the Senate Committee on Foreign Relations, 93 Cong. 1 sess. (1973), p. 15.

Table 4-1. Ground-Launched TNW Deployed with U.S. Forces in Europe

Name of system	Number deployed[a]	Range (nautical miles)	Yield (kilotons)	Dual-capable	Initial operational capability
Honest John	36	4.5– 22.0	20.0	Yes	1953
Sergeant	36	2.4– 84.0	Low	Yes	1962
Lance	36	2.6– 70.0	1.0–100.0	No	1973
Pershing	108	96.0–390.0	60.0–400.0	No	1962
Nike-Hercules	144	1.0– 20.0	1.0	Yes	1958
M-109 155-mm howitzer	326[b]	9.0	Low	Yes	1962
M-110 8-inch howitzer	360	8.0	Low	Yes	1964
ADM	Unknown	1.0– 3.0	Low	No	1950s

Sources: Author's estimates based on data appearing in International Institute for Strategic Studies, *The Military Balance, 1972–73,* and *The Military Balance, 1973–74* (London: IISS, 1972, 1973); T. N. Dupuy and Wendell Blanchard, *The Almanac of World Military Power* (2nd ed., R. R. Bowker Company, 1972); Trevor Cliffe, *Military Technology and the European Balance,* Adelphi Papers, 89 (London: International Institute for Strategic Studies, 1972); R. T. Pretty and D. H. R. Archer (eds.), *Jane's Weapon Systems, 1971–72* (McGraw-Hill, 1972); and Richard Rhodes, "Los Alamos Revisited," *Harper's,* vol. 248 (March 1974).
a. Nominal estimates, based on the number of units deployed.
b. Combined U.S. and allied deployments.

are stationed in England), as well as about 80 Navy A-6s and A-7A/B/Es aboard two carriers in the Mediterranean. All four types are dual-capable and may be considered semistrategic systems, since their operational radii vary from 750 miles for the F-4 to 1,500 miles for the F-111.[4] A varying portion of these aircraft, along with some West European planes, missiles, and submarines are constantly nuclear-loaded and maintained on Quick Reaction Alert. Nuclear bombs carried by these aircraft range from about 0.1 kiloton to over 1 megaton, though the majority of these bombs are of the free-fall variety and are in the high kiloton range.

Any review, however brief, of U.S. air-delivered TNW capabilities in Europe must include potential reinforcements located outside the European theater because the mobility of tactical aircraft permits their rapid redeployment from one region to another. As shown in Table 4-2, should circumstances require it, present U.S. deployments of nuclear-capable tactical aircraft in the European area could be almost tripled within thirty days; reinforcements could include as many as fifteen squadrons (containing about 360 planes) of F-4s and nine squadrons of F-111s. Also transferable from U.S. bases within the same period are about 500 nuclear-capable F-105D/B and F-100C/D aircraft drawn from the U.S.A.F. Reserve and the Air National Guard. Carrier-borne aircraft, of course, would be slower in arriving; and their ability to reach Central and East European targets would be severely constrained by the likelihood that carrier task forces would be compelled to operate at substantial distances offshore in order to avoid Soviet land-based aviation.

Although impressive in number, it is highly unlikely that more than a small fraction of U.S. dual-capable tactical aircraft would ever be employed in a nuclear role in a European conflict, given the certainty of tremendous demands for interdiction and conventional fire support for engaged ground forces even in a war that had crossed the nuclear threshold. Nonetheless, the sheer magnitude of their aggregate nuclear potential has had a dramatic impact on Soviet defense planning. Soviet eagerness to include forward-based systems in arms control discussions undoubtedly reflects uneasiness over the presence in Europe of large numbers of U.S. tactical aircraft capable of reaching the USSR. This is evident not only in Soviet arms control posture but also in the im-

4. These figures represent maximum-range nuclear flight profiles based on a payload of a single 2,000-pound bomb and maximum fuel. Actual mission profiles, of course, would vary widely depending on target criteria, target defenses, range, weather, and other factors. "Conventional" radii would necessarily be shorter because of the greater weight and drag associated with nonnuclear ordnance.

Table 4-2. U.S. Nuclear-Capable Tactical Aircraft Available for European Contingencies

Source	Type	Number now deployed in Europe	Deployable in Europe by M + 30[a]	Strike radius (nautical miles)	Maximum speed[b]	Initial operational capability
U.S.A.F.	F-4	528	888	700	2.4	1962
	F-111	72	288	1,500	2.2	1967
	F-105D/B[c]	0	158	1,000	2.2	1960
	F-100C/D[c]	0	352	600	0.9	1955
U.S.N.	A-6	24	48[d]	900	0.9	1956
	A-7A/B/E	60	120[d]	900	0.9	1966
Total		684	1,854			

Sources: Author's estimates based on data appearing in International Institute for Strategic Studies, *The Military Balance, 1972–73* and *The Military Balance, 1973–74*; Dupuy and Blanchard, *The Almanac of World Military Power* (1972); Pretty and Archer, *Jane's Weapon Systems, 1971–72*; and John W. R. Taylor (ed.), *Jane's All the World's Aircraft, 1973* (McGraw-Hill, 1972).

a. Cumulative total 30 days following the decision to mobilize.
b. Mach number.
c. Drawn from U.S.A.F. Reserve and Air National Guard.
d. Represents the reinforcement of the Sixth Fleet by two additional carriers.

**Table 4-3. Distances to Soviet Territory and Major Cities
from U.S. and Allied Air Bases in NATO Europe**
Nautical miles

Region	Air base	Distance to closest Pact territory	Distance to Soviet territory	Distance to closest major Soviet city
Northern	Tromso AB, Norway	300	300	400 (Murmansk)
Flank	Karup AB, Denmark	175	375	400 (Kaliningrad)
NATO	Ahlhorn AB, Germany	75	400	425 (Kaliningrad)
North	Soesterberg AB, Netherlands	175	550	575 (Kaliningrad)
	Bentwaters AB, U.K.	375	700	725 (Kaliningrad)
NATO	Beauvechain AB, Belgium	175	650	700 (L'Vov)
Center	Rhein-Main AB, Germany	75	500	550 (L'Vov)
NATO	Furstenfeldbruck AB, Germany	100	450	500 (L'Vov)
South	Aviano AB, Italy	175	450	550 (Chernoutsy)
Southern	Brindisi AB, Italy	60	525	650 (Odessa)
Flank	Thessaloniki AB, Greece	75	300	475 (Odessa)
	Eskisehir AB, Turkey	275	275	325 (Sevastopol)
	Merzifon AB, Turkey	200	200	225 (Sevastopol)

mense size (3,000 aircraft) of the Soviet Air Defense Command, which has remained essentially unchanged despite the reduction of the U.S. bomber forces in recent years.

The strategic potential of many forward-deployed U.S. tactical aircraft is undeniable. It can be grasped by comparing the operational radii of certain aircraft shown in Table 4-2 to the distances to Soviet territory and cities from selected U.S. and allied air bases in NATO Europe, shown in Table 4-3. Because of the relatively long ranges involved and the probability of encountering stiff air defenses, the number of U.S. aircraft that could actually reach targets inside the USSR is highly dependent on the locations of their bases. As currently positioned, most land-based tactical aircraft are not optimally deployed to strike the Soviet Union; moreover, carrier aircraft, if unrefueled, would have to launch from the Eastern Mediterranean—well within range of Soviet land-based aviation. On the other hand, a redeployment of aircraft to the NATO flank areas would threaten most of western Russia, including many Soviet medium- and intermediate-range ballistic missile (MR/IRBM) sites.[5] The benefit of air refueling would, of course, extend

5. Ranges of various categories of missiles are defined here as follows: medium-range ballistic missiles (MRBM)—0–1,500 miles; intermediate-range ballistic missiles (IRBM)—1,500–3,600 miles; intercontinental ballistic missiles (ICBM)—3,600 miles and over.

strike radii, although the availability of tankers would be limited if strategic forces were simultaneously placed on maximum alert status.

Yet, despite the present location of most U.S. aircraft in the United Kingdom and NATO Center and the presumption of at least an initial phase of conventional combat, the tactical air fleet that could be assembled in Europe by M + 30 would still possess a significant long-range nuclear strike capability. Furthermore, the aircraft most suited for strategic employment are also those best configured for deep interdiction in a conventional mode and thus might be more likely to be withheld during the early phases of a NATO conflict.

The successful use of air-delivered TNW in close support of engaged friendly forces is a function of delivery accuracy and yield and requires effective air-to-ground coordination. Close support could, of course, be provided by the present tactical air fleet, but nuclear surface-to-surface missiles and artillery are probably more appropriate for this task.

Most first-line U.S. aircraft have the ability to carry several nuclear bombs, although targeting restrictions, flight performance, and the availability of weapons suggest that a majority would actually carry only one. The F-111, with an internal bomb bay and superior avionics for navigation and delivery, might well carry more. A variety of bombs and air-to-ground guided missiles are available, many with selectable yields. For example, the B-61, one of the newer bombs, is reported to have several yields, selectable by a dial on the bomb, ranging up to over 200 kilotons.[6] The B-61 represents a vast improvement over the Nagasaki-style bombs of the 1950s, but is still a far cry from the very limited yields and effects envisioned for the next generation of miniaturized TNW, discussed in Chapter 7.

Delivery accuracies are an essential factor in estimating "target kill probability" and collateral damage. Airborne nuclear accuracies by visual delivery are about the same as those for conventional ordnance—in the neighborhood of 100 feet Circular Error Probable (CEP).[7] Radar, a more likely delivery mode, is generally much less accurate, depending on the type of target-acquisition and delivery avionics used. Thus, present delivery accuracies suggest that extremely low-yield weapons might prove ineffectual on some targets, and that to avoid substantial collateral damage, bombs carried by the present tactical fleet might be limited to the very low kiloton range. On the other hand,

6. Walter Pincus, "Why More Nukes?" *New Republic* (Feb. 9, 1974), p. 11.
7. The radius of a circle into which 50 percent of all deliveries would be expected to fall.

accuracies averaging less than 10 feet CEP can and have been achieved through the use of "smart" bombs,[8] which, if combined with very small yields, would greatly increase the battlefield utility of present tactical aircraft when employed in a tactical nuclear mode.

Sea-Based Systems

Virtually all U.S. sea-based TNW are designed for defensive surface or subsurface naval operations; none are suitable for employment against land targets. Sea-based systems include the *Asroc, Subroc,* and *Astor* torpedoes and depth charges as well as the *Talos* and *Terrier* surface-to-air missiles. Planned for procurement in 1975 is the *Harpoon* cruise missile, designed to enhance the U.S. Navy's antiship capabilities. The *Harpoon* may be launched from either surface units, submarines, or tactical aircraft. With the exception of the *Terrier* and the *Astor* (Mark 45) torpedo, all systems are dual-capable. Low kiloton yields are characteristic of all these weapons, and ranges vary from 0.1 to 12 miles for the *Asroc* to about 90 miles for the *Talos*.

Dependent Allied Capabilities

European allies of the United States possess a large number of tactical nuclear delivery systems, most of them of U.S. design. However, the nuclear warheads for those of U.S. design, although earmarked for allied use, remain under the physical control of U.S. forces on the continent. Only France and Great Britain possess "national" delivery systems *and* nuclear warheads outside of U.S. custody.

Ground-Launched Systems

Over 3,000 U.S. European-deployed warheads for ground-launched TNW are intended for allied use. These include warheads for all the systems, except for ADM, listed in Table 4-1. In addition, France has begun deployment of its own dual-capable *Pluton* SSM (with a range

---

8. "Smart" bomb is shorthand for improved guidance system. These systems fall into three general categories: (1) reflected laser energy for homing, (2) electro-optical devices to assist visual delivery, and (3) television guidance from within the cockpit. Many of these guidance systems also may be used by ground-launched weapons.

of 6 to 72 miles and a reported yield of 20 kilotons), the only ground-launched TNW in Western Europe that is not of U.S. design. The *Nike-Hercules* SAM and the 150-mm and 8-inch howitzers account for the bulk of allied ground-launched systems dependent on U.S. warheads, a large proportion of which are deployed in West Germany, although substantial numbers are located in the Netherlands, Italy, Greece, and Turkey. Indeed, the Federal Republic is the only European member of NATO whose forces possess *Sergeant* and *Pershing* SSM.

Tactical Air Systems

Approximately 900 nuclear-capable tactical aircraft of U.S. design are assigned to operational squadrons of allied air forces. These include the F-4, F-100, and a large number of F-104 *Starfighters*. Greece also maintains three squadrons of obsolete nuclear-capable F-84Fs. Another 400 planes of British and French design, with operational radii varying from 500 miles for the *Mirage* IIIE/B/5 to 1,600 miles for the *Canberra* B, are present in the air forces of France, Great Britain, and Belgium. These include, in addition to the aforementioned, the *Buccaneer, Mystère* IV-A, and *Entendard* IV-M.[9] Great Britain also continues to maintain about 100 *Vulcan* B-2 bombers. These aircraft, once the primary repository of Britain's strategic deterrent (now located in four *Polaris* submarines), are presently designated for tactical use, and an unknown number are maintained on QRA.

Except for some British and French planes, allied deployments of nuclear-capable tactical aircraft are located in their home countries. A number of British and French aircraft are aboard carriers that normally operate in the Atlantic, Mediterranean, and the North Sea; sizable contingents of British planes are also based in West Germany, Malta, and Cyprus.

Command and Control of U.S. TNW

All U.S. nuclear warheads in Europe, including those designated for employment by allied forces, are under the physical control of U.S. forces on the continent. The disposition, movement, and release of earmarked warheads are governed by specific agreements between the U.S. and various European allies. Although the details of these agreements

9. The French *Entendard* IV-M is a carrier-based aircraft with a maximum range of 800 miles.

are largely secret, their broad outlines are known. For example, only the President of the United States may release U.S. warheads for either U.S. or allied use, and in "no case, according to U.S. officials, are nuclear weapons present without the local government having been told."[10]

An integral feature of the command and control of all U.S. nuclear weapons are the so-called Permissive Action Link (PAL) procedures. Originally intended as locking devices for the physical control of nuclear ordnance, PAL has evolved into a management philosophy whose primary objective is to prevent *all* forms of unauthorized use of nuclear weapons. The underlying principle of PAL is that any human involvement with nuclear weapons must be undertaken by at least two persons simultaneously, thereby reducing the chance of irrational or subversive acts.

Disposition

The locations of U.S. TNW in Europe are determined by the Supreme Allied Commander Europe (SACEUR) in agreement with appropriate U.S. military commands and the government of the country concerned. According to a recent Senate Staff Report, as of July 31, 1973, U.S. land-based nuclear warheads were "stored at over 100 special ammunition sites" in Europe, one-third of which are believed designated for use by U.S. forces, with the remainder earmarked for allied employment.[11] TNW to be used by tactical aircraft are usually located on or near bases where those aircraft are stationed.[12] The storage program is under the supervision of the U.S. European Command. Custody of all weapons is maintained by special U.S. custodial teams, whose work is regulated by a complex set of procedures designed to insure the physical safety of the weapons and to prevent their unauthorized release.

Movement

Peacetime movement of weapons for operational purposes may be authorized only by the Commander-in-Chief, U.S. Forces in Europe,

10. Report on Tactical Nuclear Weapons by Senator Gaylord Nelson, *Congressional Record,* July 20, 1971, p. S11626.

11. *U.S. Security Issues in Europe,* p. 14.

12. "In a typical NATO nuclear warhead storage site . . . the weapons are kept in storage igloos and, in some cases, in the maintenance and assembly building. The site is surrounded by a double perimeter fence which is floodlit at night. The igloos and the maintenance and assembly building are equipped with an alert system which is monitored by U.S. military personnel who also control normal entry to the site. The perimeter is guarded by forces of the user country who are responsible for security from the fence out" (ibid., p. 15).

who is also the NATO SACEUR. During an alert, weapons apparently may be moved without his authorization, although they must remain under U.S. control. In all cases movement is handled by U.S. custodial teams, several members of which must validate the order to move. Even when a warhead has been joined with its delivery vehicle (as is constantly the case with U.S. and European aircraft kept on QRA), it remains subject to a multiple control whereby a number of individuals must confirm the validity of any order to launch or fire.

Consultation Prior to Use

A request to employ nuclear weapons may originate either from a NATO commander or from a member government. According to present NATO guidelines, any request must be delivered immediately to NATO governments and to the Defense Planning Committee (DPC), which encompasses all members except France. It is expected that the DPC would review the merits of the proposed use of nuclear weapons and provide an opportunity for member governments to voice their opinions. These views would then be conveyed to the nuclear power concerned (which almost certainly would be the United States), on whose authority the final decision would rest. That decision would then be immediately forwarded to Allied governments, appropriate NATO commanders, and the North Atlantic Council. The official estimate of the length of time necessary to complete this consultation process is secret, although some observers have concluded that the potential for Allied disunity in the face of demands to use nuclear weapons could easily render the procedure a lengthy if not a paralyzing one.

SACEUR thus would not be allowed to employ nuclear weapons without direct consultations with NATO member governments and the DPC. However, no NATO body possesses the authority to order SACEUR to use nuclear weapons; such an order can be given only by the President of the United States (or, for British and French weapons, the British Prime Minister and French President, respectively). And the President, before releasing weapons or ordering their use in Europe, is obligated to consult *only* if circumstances permit it.

Of significance is the fact that, technically, the President cannot order SACEUR . . . to fire a nuclear weapon; he can only release the weapon to him (*although he can unilaterally direct the same commander, in his national capacity as commander of U.S. Forces in Europe, to employ nuclear weapons*). SACEUR would then regard the President's decision to release a nuclear weapon to him as a valid reflection of NATO's collective interest and will, although the release is not a command so that SACEUR would still retain discretion as to whether or not to fire the weapon (emphasis added).[13]

Strategy and Doctrine

TNW comprise a major element of the strategy of flexible (or graduated) response adopted by the Kennedy administration in 1962 and formally endorsed by NATO in 1967. Proponents of this strategy, which remains the doctrinal foundation of Western European defense, believe that the presence of U.S. TNW on the continent not only enhances deterrence of nuclear and major conventional aggression but also serves to provide a link between conventional defense, should it fail, and U.S. willingness to employ its strategic deterrent on behalf of its European allies. By providing nuclear options more appropriate to contingencies that might arise in Europe, TNW strengthen the U.S. nuclear guarantee.

Conditions for Use

In Chapter 3 the basic guidelines governing the use of U.S. TNW in Europe laid down by Secretary of Defense Robert S. McNamara in 1963 were reviewed. These guidelines continue to define the broad outlines of U.S. and NATO policy on the subject and have been reaffirmed by Secretary of Defense James R. Schlesinger. "We deploy nuclear weapons to Europe," he recently stated before two Senate Foreign Relations Subcommittees, "to deter use of nuclear weapons by the Pact" and "to contain and halt major conventional aggression."[14]

Although the necessity of a nuclear riposte to a nuclear attack has never been questioned, the strategy of a NATO first use of TNW in response to nonnuclear aggression that NATO's conventional forces appeared unable to stop has generated considerable controversy. While the U.S. generally favors resort to nuclear weapons only as a last resort, many European governments (and particularly West Germany), believing that peacetime talk of delayed use weakens deterrence, tend to support a declaratory policy of prompt if not instant nuclear response

13. Ibid., p. 20.
14. Statement by Secretary of Defense James R. Schlesinger before the Senate Foreign Relations Subcommittees on U.S. Security Agreements and Commitments Abroad and Arms Control, International Law and Organization (April 4, 1974; processed), pp. 3, 4.

to any form of aggression. The controversy stems largely from the ambiguity of the concept of "Europe in danger of being overrun";[15] that is, what constitutes a "failure" of conventional defense? This ambiguity reflects the deliberate attempt of NATO planners to impose upon their Soviet and East European counterparts a high degree of tactical uncertainty. Thus, U.S. and NATO pronouncements have pointedly avoided attempts to establish specific criteria for conventional failure (for example, a breach of Rhine defenses); such criteria may, in any event, be impossible to formulate in peacetime.

Modes of Employment

Once the decision were made to use nuclear weapons, their employment would be regulated by existing operational plans drawn up by the Nuclear Activities Branch of Supreme Headquarters Allied Powers Europe (SHAPE). The Nuclear Activities Branch operates under a set of U.S. and NATO guidelines contained in a document known as "Concepts for the Role of Theater Nuclear Strike Forces in Allied Command Europe." This document is supplemented by SHAPE's General Strike Plan (GSP), which delineates two basic modes of nuclear warfare—selective use and general nuclear response.[16] The former is clearly the preferred alternative. Both U.S. presidential approval and intra-NATO consultation must precede either selective or general use, although the GSP provides SACEUR with the capability for deliberate escalation with which he can expand the scope or increase the intensity of combat in order to strengthen his defensive effort or to insure the survival of his forces within the scope of authority the President has authorized him to use.[17]

SELECTIVE USE. Selective use of TNW is designed to serve either tactical or demonstrative purposes and represents the kind of limited

15. Testimony of Secretary of Defense Robert S. McNamara, *Department of Defense Appropriations for 1964,* Hearings before a Subcommittee of the House Committee on Appropriations, 88 Cong. 1 sess. (1963), pt. 1, p. 102.

16. Weapon systems available for nuclear strikes under the GSP include land- and sea-based aircraft, sea-based missiles, and *Pershing* missiles, which in wartime are to be assigned by NATO countries to SACEUR. Remaining land-based systems do not fall under the category of strike forces, although they would remain available for use at SACEUR's discretion.

17. *U.S. Security Issues in Europe,* p. 21.

tactical nuclear war most often envisaged by U.S. planners. The essence of selective use is the controlled employment of limited numbers of discriminating TNW against military targets with the explicit aim of inflicting as little collateral damage as possible. The lowest end of the selective use spectrum is represented by what one observer has called a single "warning or so-called shot-across-the-bow" designed solely to demonstrate NATO's resolve to carry conventional conflict across the nuclear threshold should aggression continue.[18] The next level of response would be characterized by multiple strikes on discrete and relatively proximate military targets whose destruction could be accomplished by low-yield TNW. The object of this type of response would be both to demonstrate willingness to wage an expanded nuclear war and to confer tactical advantages upon defending forces. Should aggression remain unchecked, however, NATO strategic guidance envisages an ever-widening employment of nuclear weapons up to and including theater nuclear war—selective only in the sense that it would be conducted in the absence of a strategic exchange.

GENERAL NUCLEAR RESPONSE. Under a general nuclear response TNW would be employed *in conjunction with* strikes delivered by U.S. strategic forces against targets in both Europe and the Soviet Union. An existing Single Integrated Operations Plan designed for such an eventuality would determine the synchronized employment of all nuclear strike forces, both theater and strategic. Since the presumption of a general nuclear response is the existence or imminence of all-out nuclear war, the controlled employment of force characteristic of selective use is not expected to be an important factor.

The Prospect of Premature French Use

The ability of a U.S. President to determine the character and timing of a NATO tactical nuclear response in Europe is compromised by the existence of French TNW independent of American authority. The possibility of the United States being dragged into a nuclear conflict as a result of an early French nuclear riposte is a real one. Indeed, a number of factors strongly suggests that French tactical nuclear posture has been deliberately designed to compel employment of U.S. TNW on French

18. Morton H. Halperin, *Defense Strategies for the Seventies* (Little, Brown, 1971), p. 105.

rather than U.S. or allied terms: France's public ridicule of the reliability of the American nuclear guarantee; bitter Gaullist resentment of U.S. domination of nuclear planning within NATO; French lack of faith in conventional defense; and the Fifth Republic's announced policy of using nuclear weapons—regardless of allied preferences—in response to any Soviet attack that threatened France.

The consequences of French posture for NATO's capacity to sustain a unified and well-coordinated defense of Western Europe have not gone unnoticed:

France by its policies reduces the possibility of a conventional defense, and significantly lowers the nuclear threshold . . .

French tactical nuclear weapons, if used in the midst of a conventional engagement between NATO . . . and Warsaw Pact forces, could force the U.S. into a nuclear war. The Alliance has been able to tolerate this bad situation during the period of U.S. nuclear superiority, but strategic parity makes the French position totally at odds with the best interest of NATO and stability in Central Europe. The French position is also incompatible with a long-term U.S. commitment in Europe and the Alliance must find ways of resolving this dangerous situation.[19]

Costs of the U.S. Deployment in Europe

The costs of maintaining U.S. tactical nuclear weapons in Europe are difficult to assess because many of the pertinent data are either classified or otherwise hidden from public view. For example, the costs of producing nuclear materials and developing, producing, and testing nuclear warheads, all of which are borne by the Atomic Energy Commission (AEC), are included in aggregate accounts that do not distinguish between tactical and strategic weapons. Moreover, the number of warheads provided annually to the military services by the AEC—to say nothing of the number allocated to European contingencies—has never been disclosed publicly.

Another problem is methodological: which weapon systems may justifiably be included as part of the cost of the U.S. tactical nuclear deployment in Europe? To incorporate all nuclear-capable delivery systems ignores the more important contribution most of these weapons make to NATO's conventional deterrent. Indeed, it is the author's judgment that no dual-capable systems should be included because the num-

---

19. *Policy, Troops, and the NATO Alliance,* Report of Senator Sam Nunn to the Senate Committee on Armed Services (Government Printing Office, 1974), p. 3.

ber deployed is a function primarily of perceived requirements for conventional defense. The only exception might be the three squadrons of F-111s based in the United Kingdom; although dual-capable, their main role in Europe is often cited as a nuclear one and many F-111s are maintained on QRA.

Certain costs directly associated with the U.S. tactical nuclear deployment in Europe, however, are clearly identifiable. For example, the program acquisition costs (which include procurement, research and development, and military construction costs) and direct operating expenses of delivery systems justified solely on the basis of nuclear capability, although variable, lend themselves to estimation. These expenses would include the pay and other compensation for the approximately 35,000 U.S. troops in Europe that are assigned to the USAREUR Missile Forces and to other units that operate, maintain, and safeguard the scores of nuclear warhead storage sites on the continent.[20] As shown in Table 4-4, these costs in fiscal 1975 totaled $614 million, of which $370 million was related to the cost of manpower. Not counted in Table 4-4 are the costs of manpower providing support to deployed tactical nuclear units—for example, recruiting, training, and maintaining the health of their personnel. By conservative estimate these costs would total at least an additional $400 million.

Program acquisition costs for the *Lance* and *Pershing* missiles (minus their warheads), which are the only U.S. TNW in Europe—except for ADM[21]—that are exclusively nuclear-capable, totaled about $100 million in fiscal 1975.[22] Virtually no reliable information is available on the costs of nuclear warheads, including those for the *Lance* and *Pershing*. Enthoven, however, has suggested an average of $500,000 per warhead for tactical nuclear delivery systems,[23] a figure that is borne out by the author's calculations. This estimate is also in line with the AEC's unsuccessful fiscal 1974 budget request for $904 million to develop and produce some 2,000 new nuclear shells for the 8-inch

20. This figure includes the 23,000 men currently assigned to the USAREUR Missile Forces and an estimated additional 12,000 men involved in the operation and maintenance of warhead storage sites, two-thirds (8,000) of whom are believed to be U.S. Army personnel.

21. Costs associated with ADM do not appear in Table 4-4 because of insufficient data; they are probably not very significant since ADM are comparatively cheap TNW and very few are thought to have been procured in recent years.

22. Schlesinger, *op. cit.,* pp. 113-14, and *Department of Defense FY 1975 Budget Program Acquisition Costs,* pp. 32–33.

23. A Statement by Alain C. Enthoven on U.S. Military Forces in Europe before the Senate Committee on Foreign Relations (March 14, 1974; processed), p. 18.

Table 4-4. Selected Direct Costs of Maintaining the U.S. Tactical Nuclear Deployment in Europe, Fiscal Year 1975
Millions of FY 1975 dollars

Cost category	Aggregate cost
Manpower[a]	
USAREUR missile forces (23,000)	241
Other personnel costs (12,000)	132
Subtotal	373
Program acquisition[b]	
Delivery vehicles	
Lance (194)	68
Pershing[c] (88)	32
Warheads[d]	
Lance (194)	97
Pershing (88)	44
Subtotal	241
Total	614

Sources: Author's estimates based on data drawn from Secretary of Defense James R. Schlesinger, *Annual Defense Department Report, FY 1975*, pp. 113–14; *Department of Defense FY 1975 Budget Program Acquisition Costs*, pp. 32–33; and *The Budget of the United States Government Fiscal Year 1975, Appendix*, pp. 265–355, 753–59.

a. Manpower costs were calculated by multiplying the number of "tactical nuclear" troops (35,000) by appropriate fiscal 1975 per capita Military Personnel costs for active personnel. U.S. Army personnel, which include those assigned to the USAREUR Missile Forces and about two-thirds of those in "Other personnel costs," represented in fiscal 1975 a per capita Military Personnel expenditure of about $10,500; the figure for Air Force personnel, who are believed to comprise only about one-third of the total in "Other personnel costs," was estimated at $12,000.

b. Includes procurement, research and development, and military construction costs.

c. Modernization costs for the *Pershing I* and *IA* systems.

d. Assumes one warhead per delivery vehicle and a cost of $500,000 per warhead.

howitzers,[24] with a cost per warhead of about $452,000. Using the figure of $500,000 and assuming the procurement of one warhead per missile, since neither the *Lance* nor the *Pershing* are retrievable systems, the aggregate fiscal 1975 procurement costs for *Lance* and *Pershing* warheads were estimated at about $150 million.

It is important to recognize that the total of $614 million given in Table 4-4 is the sum of only selected direct costs and so represents only a fraction of the total real cost of maintaining the present U.S. tactical nuclear posture in Europe. For example, not included in the table are the costs of sea-based systems, routine upgrading of nuclear ordnance, a host of ongoing tactical nuclear research and development efforts such as the *Pershing II* and *SAM-D* programs as well as those related to the miniaturization of TNW, and manpower supporting deployed tactical nuclear forces. Together, these costs annually run into the billions of dollars, most of which are justified by the perceived necessity of maintaining a U.S. tactical nuclear deployment in Europe.

24. Lloyd Norman, "The Reluctant Dragon: NATO's Fears and the Need for New Nuclear Weapons," *Army*, vol. 24 (February 1974), p. 20.

CHAPTER FIVE

ASYMMETRIES BETWEEN U.S. AND SOVIET TACTICAL NUCLEAR POSTURES

The purpose of this chapter is to identify and explore those asymmetries between U.S. and Soviet tactical nuclear postures that have implications for U.S. TNW and the projected manner of their employment. These asymmetries are present both in the character of U.S. and Soviet TNW and in the respective doctrines that govern their use.

Soviet Capabilities

The USSR is believed to maintain about 3,500 tactical nuclear warheads in the European area.[1] Although a large portion of Soviet delivery systems are deployed with Soviet forces in Eastern Europe, many if not most nuclear warheads may be retained inside the USSR. The deployment encompasses air-to-surface missiles, surface-to-surface missiles (SSM), nuclear-configured tactical aircraft, and some sea-based systems. The Soviet Union is also reported to have a dual-capable 8-inch howitzer. Soviet forces are not known to possess either tactical nuclear surface-to-air missiles or atomic demolition munitions.

As shown in Table 5-1, yields of Soviet TNW, most of which are missiles, range from several kilotons to several megatons, and thus on balance are distinctly more destructive than U.S. weapons. The majority of Soviet TNW exceed 20 kilotons, with some 600 systems in the 500–3,000 kiloton range. Indeed, the available data strongly suggest that the USSR possesses no warheads with yields less than 5 kilotons. Moreover, Soviet delivery systems are demonstrably less accurate than NATO's.[2]

On the other hand, Soviet ground-launched TNW are less vulnerable,

---

1. International Institute for Strategic Studies, *The Military Balance 1973–1974* (London: IISS, 1973), p. 91.

2. Martin J. Miller, Jr., "Soviet Nuclear Tactics," *Ordnance,* vol. 14 (May–June 1970), p. 627.

Table 5-1. Distribution of Soviet Ground-Launched and Sea-Based Tactical Nuclear Weapons by Estimated Yield[a]

Less than 20 kilotons		*20–500 kilotons*		*500–1,000 kilotons*	*1000–3,000 kilotons*
8-inch howitzer (100)		SCUD-B	(75)[b]	SKEAN (100)	SANDAL (500)
SCUD-A	(50)[b]	FROG 6-7	(75)		
SCUD-B	(75)[c]	SHADDOCK	(560)		
FROG 2-5	(400)[d]	SCALEBOARD	(100)		
		SARK/SERB	(85)		
Subtotals:	(625)		(1020)	(100)	(500)

a. Numbers in parentheses are estimated number of systems.
b. Assumes SCUD inventory to be two-thirds of SCUD-B inventory.
c. Assumes one-half SCUD-B inventory has yields selectable from low to high kiloton range.
d. Assumes one-third of FROG inventory to be FROG 6-7 models. Older models are assumed to have fixed yield, newer FROGs to have selectable yields.

according to some analysts, because "unlike the American tactical missile systems, the Soviets have attempted to incorporate all missile launch operations into a single transporter/launcher vehicle."[3] As for the approximately 700 Soviet medium- and intermediate-range ballistic missiles (MR/IRBM) targeted on Europe, because they are located in the USSR they must be considered completely invulnerable in all circumstances short of a strategic nuclear war. Soviet and Pact nuclear-capable tactical aircraft are certainly less vulnerable than NATO's if for no other reason than that they are dispersed over a much larger number of airfields in both the USSR and Eastern Europe.[4]

A significant aspect of the Soviet TNW in Europe is that they are the only such weapons in the Warsaw Pact. Although European allies of the USSR do retain a number of inherently dual-capable SSM and tactical aircraft, they do not possess nuclear weapons, for the Soviets have always been careful to supply their allies with equipment of extremely limited offensive potential. More important is the absence of any evidence to suggest that the USSR would make TNW available to Eastern European countries even in wartime. The contingency plans for the transfer of U.S. warheads to allied delivery systems that characterize NATO's tactical nuclear posture are in sharp contrast to the Soviet determination to retain an absolute monopoly of all nuclear weapons

3. Ibid.
4. For example, Neville Brown states that in "East Germany, Czechoslovakia, and Poland there are over 220 airfields entirely suitable for high performance [tactical] aircraft and also 140 lesser ones. Yet NATO's designated airfields number no more than one-third of this combined total" (*European Security 1972–1980* [London: Royal United Services Institute for Defense Studies, 1972], p. 124).

Table 5-2. Soviet Ground-Launched Tactical Nuclear Weapons[a]

NATO code name	Number deployed	Probable location	Yield	Dual capable?	Range (nautical miles)
FROG 2-7[b]	600	Eastern Europe	Multikiloton	Yes	4–50
SCUD-A		Eastern Europe	Multikiloton	Yes	48–60
	200		Kiloton-		
SCUD-B		Eastern Europe	megaton[c]	Yes	48–185
SHADDOCK[d]	100[e]	USSR only	Multikiloton	No	60–300
SCALEBOARD	100	USSR[f]	Multikiloton[c]	?	4–480
SANDAL		USSR only	Megaton	No	900–1,000
	600[e]		Kiloton-		
SKEAN		USSR only	megaton	No	1,750–2,000
8-inch howitzer	100	Eastern Europe	Multikiloton	Yes	16

Sources: Author's estimates based on data appearing in International Institute for Strategic Studies, *The Military Balance, 1972–1973* and *The Military Balance, 1973–1974* (London: IISS, 1972, 1973); T. N. Dupuy and Wendell Blanchard, *The Almanac of World Military Power* (2nd ed., R. R. Bowker Company, 1972); Trevor Cliffe, *Military Technology and the European Balance*, Adelphi Papers, 89 (London: International Institute for Strategic Studies, 1972); and R. T. Pretty and D. H. R. Archer (eds.), *Jane's Weapon Systems, 1971–1972* (McGraw-Hill, 1972).

a. Represents entire estimated inventory, the bulk of which is deployed in or targeted against Europe.

b. A family of SSM representing modifications of a single basic design.

c. Selectable yields.

d. Principally a naval weapon, although some are clearly configured for use by ground forces against ground targets.

e. The SHADDOCK, SANDAL, and SKEAN deployments in the USSR represent the 700 Soviet MR/IRBM targeted on Europe that form such a prominent topic of many contemporary arms control proposals.

f. Unconfirmed reports indicate that some SCALEBOARD may be deployed in Eastern Europe.

within the Warsaw Pact. This monopoly, of course, greatly simplifies problems of command and control.

There are strong indications that the control of all Soviet missiles is highly centralized, with MR/IRBM under the command of Strategic Rocket Forces, and the theater-level SCUD and SCALEBOARD (and possibly the "battlefield" FROG batteries) under the command of the Rocket and Artillery Forces. Thus, the use of most if not all Soviet tactical nuclear missiles is probably subject to the authority of at least two military commanders.

Ground-Launched Systems

The USSR maintains about 1,700 ground-launched TNW delivery systems, of which perhaps as many as 1,400 to 1,500 are deployed in or targeted against Europe. As shown in Table 5-2, all Soviet ground-launched TNW, unlike the relatively heterogeneous U.S. deployment, are surface-to-surface missiles, with the sole exception of the 8-inch howitzer. This extraordinary emphasis on missile delivery of warheads is a function of Soviet military doctrine, which uniformly contends that "missile troops [are] the basic means for the employment of nuclear weapons in combined arms combat."[5]

Ranges of Soviet SSM vary from 4 to 50 miles for the FROG series to 1,750 to 2,000 miles for the SKEAN IRBM. Yields are generally in the multiple kiloton range, although yields of one megaton or more are attributed to most Soviet MR/IRBM, all of which, with the possible exception of some SCALEBOARD, are located inside the USSR. Some systems are dual-capable, although, as noted above, nuclear warheads for systems deployed with Soviet forces in Eastern Europe may be retained inside the USSR.

Tactical Air Systems

Table 5-3 shows that the USSR maintains at present approximately 2,400 aircraft that could be used in a tactical nuclear mode. It is highly improbable, however, that a significant fraction of these would ever be so employed. The Soviet Union's strong preference for missiles, not aircraft, as the principal means of delivering nuclear ordnance has already been noted.[6] Moreover, Soviet tactical air doctrine, the product of a traditional land-oriented military philosophy that places a premium on massive concentrations of armor and artillery, relegates tactical air forces largely to the roles of defending the Soviet homeland and countering enemy airpower over the battlefield. This defensive orientation contrasts sharply with U.S. doctrine, which attaches great importance to the achievement of theater air superiority as a prerequisite to deep interdiction.

Finally, the relative design simplicity of Soviet tactical aircraft and their probable lack of sophisticated avionics packages strongly suggest a pronounced inability to deliver ordnance with the degree of accuracy necessary for battlefield deployment of TNW. The use of Soviet tactical aircraft in the nuclear mode is likely to be confined, therefore, to theater targets, whose destruction in any event probably could be accomplished more rapidly and efficiently by the use of preferred SSM.

---

5. A. A. Sidorenko, *The Offensive (A Soviet View),* translated and published under the auspices of the United States Air Force (Government Printing Office, 1973), p. 43.

6. This preference is also reflected in the composition of Soviet strategic forces, the core of which consists of over 1,500 land-based ICBM supplemented by only about 140 obsolescent long-range bombers.

Table 5-3. Soviet Nuclear-Capable Tactical Aircraft[a]

Type	NATO code name	Number deployed	Strike radius (nautical miles)	Maximum speed[b]	Initial operational capability
MiG-21	FISHBED J	} 1350	350	2.2	1970
MiG-23	FLOGGER		600	2.4	1971
SU-7B	FITTER		600	1.7	1959
YAK-28	BREWER		500	1.1	1962
IL-28	BEAGLE		1,500	0.8	1950
TU-22	BLINDER[c]	260	700	1.5	1962
TU-16	BADGER A/B/C[d]	800	1,700	0.8	1955

Sources: Author's estimates based on data appearing in International Institute for Strategic Studies, *The Military Balance, 1972–1973* and *The Military Balance, 1973–1974;* Dupuy and Blanchard, *The Almanac of World Military Power* (1972); Pretty and Archer, *Jane's Weapon Systems, 1971–1972*; and John W. R. Taylor (ed.), *Jane's All the World's Aircraft, 1973* (McGraw-Hill, 1973).

a. Represents entire estimated inventory.
b. Mach number.
c. Includes units in naval aviation forces.
d. Includes about 300 units in naval aviation forces.

Sea-Launched Systems

In addition to ground-launched and air-delivered TNW, the USSR maintains over 500 SSM aboard about 115 naval vessels, mostly submarines. Ranges of Soviet sea-launched systems vary from 100 to 300 miles for the SHADDOCK to up to 650 miles for SARK. Designed primarily for antiship operations, most of these SSM could be employed directly, although with substantial loss of accuracy, against ground targets in Europe, given the proximity to the continent of most major Soviet naval deployments.

Strategy and Doctrine

Perhaps the most important asymmetries between Soviet and U.S. tactical nuclear postures lie in their respective nuclear doctrines. Soviet doctrine does not recognize the potential gradations of tactical nuclear warfare that are such a prominent feature of flexible response. This "insensitivity" to what Western military analysts believe are distinctions of crucial significance may well be a function of the character of the Soviet TNW arsenal, which may preclude the kind of discrete and highly discriminating employment of nuclear weapons that constitutes the fabric of NATO's tactical nuclear strategy. Indeed,

Soviet force structure raises serious doubts about their capability to fight a limited tactical nuclear war, much less one in which collateral damage and civilian casualties are to be kept to low levels. Limited nuclear wars with one side using discrete-fire techniques and the other using terrain fire are likely to be notoriously one-sided in favor of the latter. Equally important, most of the Soviets' nuclear delivery capability in Europe is based inside the Soviet Union. In short, the Soviets have neither the organization nor the force structure for a limited nuclear war fought exclusively against military targets in an engaged battle zone.[7]

The nature of Soviet TNW is certainly in keeping with the time-honored traditions of the Soviet (and before that, the Imperial Russian) Army, which has never emphasized "pinpoint accuracy and strict target selection but rather mass barrages intended to smash paths through enemy formations and rear areas for the ground units to exploit."[8] In fact, until recently, Soviet strategists resolutely maintained that any major conflict in Europe involving the United States would "develop, inevitably, into a general [nuclear] war."[9] Although subsequent doctrinal pronouncements have accepted the possibility that a war in Europe (or at least its initial phases) might be nonnuclear and have stressed that Soviet "forces must be prepared to fight without using nuclear weapons, utilizing the standard conventional 'classical' weapons,"[10] the evidence of a shift in the longstanding Soviet view that "there is no difference in the tactical and strategic use of atomic weapons"[11] is less conclusive.

Whether nuclear warfare remains indivisible for the Soviet Union is a matter of ongoing conjecture in the West. Many observers believe that the Russians do privately recognize the difference between strategic and tactical nuclear war and that public assertions of their inseparability are designed simply to enhance overall deterrence of military actions by the West. But there is no indication that the Soviets perceive *tactical* nuclear war as divisible. Soviet writings contain no recognition of potentially different levels and intensities of tactical nuclear conflict. Al-

7. Alain C. Enthoven and K. Wayne Smith, *How Much Is Enough? Shaping the Defense Program 1961–1969* (Harper and Row, 1971), p. 127.

8. Miller, "Soviet Nuclear Tactics," p. 627.

9. Marshal V. D. Sokolovskii, *Soviet Military Strategy,* translated and with an analytical introduction, annotations, and supplementary material by Hervert S. Dinerstein, Leon Gouré, and Thomas W. Wolfe. Originally published by the Military Publishing House of the Ministry of Defense of the USSR, 1962. A RAND Corporation Research Study (Prentice-Hall, 1963), p. 299.

10. Marshal I. I. Yakubovsky, "Soviet Ground Forces," *Red Star* (July 21, 1967). Reprinted in *Survival* (October 1967), p. 327.

11. Major-General N. Talenskii, "About Atomic and Conventional Weapons," *Mezhdunarodnaia zhizń* (*International Affairs*) (January 1955), p. 25.

though distinctions between "tactical" and "operational tactical" (roughly correspondent, respectively, to battlefield and theater) *weapons* are made, what "seems always to be absent . . . is any Soviet parallel with the Western schools of thought which argue that, since battlefield nuclear weapons are acknowledged to have a deterrent rather than an operational value, they should initially be used in a piecemeal and selective fashion; more as symbols of intent than as factors in the tactical balance."[12]

On the contrary, Soviet military strategy in Europe strongly emphasizes the necessity for "mass employment of nuclear weapons" once the nuclear threshold has been crossed.[13] That strategy is based not only upon the conviction that "nuclear weapons will become the basic means of destruction on the field of battle," but also upon the belief that "the side which first employs nuclear weapons with surprise can predetermine the outcome of the battle in his favor."[14] Soviet perception of TNW largely as a means of enhancing warfighting capabilities rather than deterrence is clearly reflected in recent writings on strategy.

Nuclear weapons are the most powerful means for the destruction of troops and rear area objectives. Among all other means of combat they possess the greatest force for physical and moral-psychological influence and therefore they have a decisive influence on the nature of the offensive. During the entire history of military art, no one weapon had such sudden and rapid influence on the nature of the offensive and on the conflict as a whole as did nuclear weapons. Their employment in the battle and operation permits inflicting large losses in personnel and equipment on the enemy almost instanteously [sic] destroying, paralysing, and putting out of action entire [battalions], [regiments], and even [corps], and thereby changing the relation of forces sharply in one's favor and destroying structures and other objectives as well as enemy centers of resistance and frustrating his counterattacks and counterblows. Thanks to this the troops can conduct the offensive at high rates and achieve the assigned goals in short times.[15]

In the event of major conflict in Europe, Soviet strategy calls for a massive blitzkrieg along a broad front designed to permit rapid occupation of continental Western Europe before NATO can mobilize its greater but less ready and more dispersed military potential. "Mass employment of nuclear weapons," if not in the form of a preemptive strike then certainly in response to any NATO first use, is believed to be the key to successful offensive operations. The role that TNW are expected

---

12. Brown, *European Security 1972–1980*, p. 69.
13. Sidorenko, *The Offensive*, pp. 58–61.
14. Ibid., pp. 41, 112.
15. Ibid., p. 40.

to play in Soviet offensive operations is not a supplementary but a dominant one.

. . . the Soviet conduct of a "land battle" would be based (to judge from their own pronouncements) from the outset on offensive action, with a mass nuclear strike delivered by medium range missiles and aircraft in great depth with the aim of destroying enemy ground and air forces, accompanied by a simultaneous advance by highspeed strike forces moving by day and by night, the armour in particular striking as deeply as possible into the enemy rear and "deep rear." High-speed mobile operations, together with extensive use of airborne forces, fit the "nuclear battlefield": air-dropped, airborne and helicopter-borne forces would be used to exploit the initial nuclear blow and would be used above all to keep the Soviet advance on the move. Reconnaissance would include the use of airborne forces, as well as air and electronic reporting, with motorised units thrown out in some depth for the same purpose. Present tactical training is based on making troops used to moving in irradiated areas and amidst zones of major destruction, "massive fires" brought about by nuclear weapons: the Soviet command meanwhile concentrates on speeding up troop control . . . and on implementing "flexibility."[16]

Thus, Soviet planners anticipate the widespread use of nuclear weapons and have deliberately organized their forces to operate on a battlefield dominated by them. Notions of demonstrative or limited tactical uses of TNW are not entertained in Soviet writings nor are they implied in the character of the USSR's TNW arsenal. Doctrinal emphasis on mass as opposed to discrete use of nuclear weapons stands in sharp contrast to NATO prescriptions. This prominent asymmetry has profound implications, discussed in the next chapter, for U.S. tactical nuclear posture.

16. John Erickson, *Soviet Military Power* (London: Royal United Services Institute for Defense Studies, 1971), pp. 66–67.

CHAPTER SIX

WEAKNESSES OF THE PRESENT
U.S. POSTURE

Three basic weaknesses in present U.S. tactical nuclear posture in Europe can now be identified. First, the deployment of U.S. TNW on the continent no longer confers upon NATO a clear advantage with respect to the *defense* of Western Europe, although it may enhance *deterrence* of certain forms of aggression. Second, the kind of tactical nuclear war envisaged by U.S. planners, and for which the Alliance has prepared— a conflict characterized by limited and controlled exchanges of discrete TNW—is at best improbable and at worst illusory. It is suspect because the nature of opposing Soviet TNW and doctrine virtually precludes Soviet participation in such a conflict and because of the likelihood of irresistable pressures for rapid and devastating escalation following the first use of nuclear weapons by either side. Third, present NATO doctrine, efficacious or not, is ill-served by the current deployment of weapons at the disposal of the Atlantic Alliance.

The Erosion of Warfighting Advantage

The possession of TNW bestowed on NATO a decided military advantage over the Pact as long as the Soviet Union failed to develop and deploy such weapons. The argument that Pact superiority in conventional arms, reinforced by neither TNW nor a credible strategic deterrent, could be countered by reliance on a nuclear defense was a compelling one. However, the demise in the late 1950s of NATO's monopoly of TNW terminated the prospect of a one-sided nuclear conflict and with it the expectation that the defense would be favored in a tactical nuclear war.

The judgment that NATO would not obtain a net military advantage in a two-sided use of TNW cannot, of course, be conclusively verified short of war. It continues, however, to represent the majority opinion of Western defense analysts and the scientific community,[1] including Secretary of Defense James R. Schlesinger, who recently concluded that because of the magnitude of destruction that would probably attend a mutual use of TNW, "it is not clear under what conditions the United States and its allies would possess a comparative military advantage in a tactical nuclear exchange."[2] A noted European analyst is less uncertain, arguing that the greater destructiveness of Soviet TNW and the fact that most of the fighting would take place in Western Europe mean that a "tactical nuclear defense of Europe would lead to its destruction."[3]

The impact of this erosion of warfighting significance on the deterrent value of TNW is the subject of much conjecture. The official U.S. position appears to be generally that the decline of military advantage once associated with TNW has not been accompanied by a corresponding reduction in deterrent value. However, a growing number of observers, claiming that deterrence is primarily a function of warfighting credibility, is drawing different conclusions. "To be effective . . . as a deterrent," asserts one writer, "a weapon must have a recognizable role in a conceivable future conflict. Tactical nuclear weapons have no such role."[4]

Whatever the deterrent value of U.S. TNW in Europe, there is little doubt that their mere presence, coupled with a deliberately ambiguous doctrine governing their use, does impose upon Soviet military planners a greater degree of tactical uncertainty than would otherwise be the case. No conventional Warsaw Pact invasion could avoid the constant danger of provoking a sudden nuclear counter-attack. Even if this tactical uncertainty did not deter a Pact attack, it would almost certainly compel a dispersion of invading forces as a hedge against the possible employment of nuclear weapons. Dispersion would constrain the Pact's

---

1. See, for example, Alain C. Enthoven and K. Wayne Smith, "What Forces for NATO and from Whom?" *Foreign Affairs*, vol. 47 (October 1968); John Newhouse and others, *U.S. Troops in Europe: Issues, Costs, and Choices* (Brookings Institution, 1971); P. M. S. Blackett, *Studies of War* (London: Oliver and Boyd, 1962); Philip W. Dyer, "Will Tactical Nuclear Weapons Ever Be Used?" *Political Science Quarterly*, vol. 88 (June 1973); and Pasti Nino, "NATO's Defense Strategy," *Orbis*, vol. 13 (Spring 1969).

2. *Annual Defense Department Report FY 1975, op. cit.*, p. 82.

3. Heinz Trettner, "Tactical Nuclear Weapons for Europe," *Military Review*, vol. 50 (July 1971), p. 48.

4. Dyer, "Will Tactical Nuclear Weapons Ever Be Used?" p. 215.

ability to concentrate its forces for major breakthrough and sustained penetration operations and thus would work to NATO's advantage.

On the other hand, this same tactical uncertainty might also encourage a first use of TNW by the Pact in the form of a preemptive strike. Indeed, some observers maintain that the U.S. TNW deployment in Europe, far from enhancing deterrence of aggression, virtually guarantees that aggression, if launched, will assume a predominantly nuclear character from the very outset of hostilities. Such conjecture is supported both by the battlefield environment postulated in most Soviet wargames and by Soviet military doctrine, which holds that "the side which first employs nuclear weapons with surprise can predetermine the outcome of the battle in his favor."[5]

In sum, although the warfighting credibility of U.S. TNW in Europe has substantially declined in the last two decades, the implications of that decline for the deterrent value of TNW are unclear. Such is not the case with respect to the principal political function now being served by U.S. TNW—the enhancement in European eyes of the credibility of the American commitment to European security. TNW represent for most Europeans, particularly West Germans, visible evidence of that commitment as well as a symbol of U.S. willingness to cross the atomic threshold relatively early on, with all the risks of escalation such a decision would entail. Indeed, the psychological value of TNW has perhaps grown in an era of waning European faith in both conventional defense and the credibility of the U.S. strategic deterrent.

The Chimera of Discrete Use

The U.S. image of tactical nuclear war in Europe as a conflict in which the controlled first use of limited numbers of TNW would be confined to military targets is decidedly unreal. It is unreal for a variety of reasons, not the least of which is its incompatibility with present Soviet weaponry and doctrine. It has been shown that the nature of Soviet TNW as well as prescriptions for their use would make it difficult if not impossible for the Soviet Union to make what by Western standards would be a discriminating use of TNW. The U.S. image would be realistic only if the USSR could be counted on to refrain from using nuclear

5. A. A. Sidorenko, *The Offensive (A Soviet View)* (Government Printing Office, 1973), p. 112.

weapons in a European conflict even if NATO chose otherwise—a highly unlikely prospect. On the contrary, Soviet doctrine strongly suggests that any major Pact invasion of Europe would be accompanied if not preceded by a "mass employment of nuclear weapons" designed to destroy or paralyze NATO's own tactical nuclear capabilities and deployed conventional forces. Under such circumstances, the use of surviving U.S. systems in a limited and discrete riposte probably would make little difference in the final outcome of hostilities or in the aggregate amount of collateral damage.

The question is often raised of what conceivable stake the Soviets would have in occupying a Western Europe devastated by nuclear strikes, or whether Soviet ground forces would be capable of sustained operations in or beyond areas contaminated by radiation. The answers to these queries remain largely speculative. It is worth remembering, however, that historically the USSR has rarely exhibited a reluctance to ravage territory it intended to occupy. As for the ability to linger on or beyond a nuclear battlefield, it is noteworthy that the USSR, to a far greater extent than either the United States or its NATO allies, has sought to prepare its ground forces for nuclear combat.[6] Preparation is evident in Pact wargames, most of which, unlike NATO's, are conducted in simulated nuclear environments, and in the extraordinary attention paid to protecting crews of armored fighting vehicles from the effects of radiation.

Skepticism about the possibility of a discrete tactical nuclear war in Europe is further warranted by what many observers believe to be the probability of rapid and uncontrollable escalation following any first use of nuclear weapons. U.S. tactical nuclear doctrine, like its parent strategy of flexible or graduated response, rests implicitly on (1) the assumption of rational conduct (as defined by U.S. strategists) in wartime on the part of enlightened adversaries, and (2) the assumption that both sides will perceive the same potential levels of conflict as well as the "escalatory significance" of each. Both of these suppositions have been severely challenged over the years by critics and events. As one prominent European observer has concluded, "The entire American

6. Testifying before the House Armed Services Committee in 1974, U.S. Army Chief of Staff Creighton Abrams stated that "one of the most impressive lessons" of the October war in the Middle East, and one which apparently surprised the Army, was the "sophistication, completeness, and extensiveness" of Soviet equipment's defenses against chemical, bacteriological, and radiological attack. Abrams went on to say that the United States lagged "well behind" the Soviets in this field (*New York Times,* Feb. 15, 1974).

theory [of graduated response] . . . attempts to reconstruct the manner in which a strategist would behave if, like his counterpart in economic theory, he were both intelligent and well-informed. But how many real-life chiefs of state resemble this idealized portrait? How many of them are always able to abide by the dictates of reason, at least reason defined by the theoreticians?"[7]

Even were cool, independent, and rational judgment the dominant characteristic of national decision making in peacetime (not obviously the case), such behavior would be exceedingly difficult to maintain in the "fog of war." These and other flaws in the intellectual foundation of graduated response probably accounted for the failure of that strategy in Vietnam, where repeated U.S. escalation of its combat involvement in the mid- and late 1960s failed to deter either the expansion of the war into neighboring states or continuing North Vietnamese attempts to conquer the South.

As for tactical nuclear war, Soviet military doctrine does not, as has been shown, recognize those potential gradations of violence within a realm of conflict that constitute the core of U.S. tactical nuclear doctrine. Even were this not so, wartime pressures for escalation beyond demonstrative or selective uses of TNW are likely to become irresistible.

Anyone who made use of tactical nuclear weapons on the assumption that his opponent would regard himself as bound by some kind of nuclear Queensberry rules—and therefore be inhibited from retaliating with nuclear weapons of heavier calibre—would be liable to an extremely rude awakening. Is it, for example, conceivable that an aggressor, having achieved his immediate aims thanks to a preponderance of conventional forces on the spot, would stand meekly by and watch his forces being wiped out by tactical nuclear bombardment when he had it in his power to inflict unacceptable damage by the use of strategic nuclear weapons?[8]

Although it is not obvious that the use of TNW in a European conflict would automatically lead to a strategic exchange between the United States and the USSR, "neither side would be clear as to what its implications were. Both sides would probably ask themselves whether this meant that central war, either immediately or in the short run, had become inevitable. In this way the use of tactical nuclear weapons . . . would probably substantially increase the pressures towards preemption and might set off a spiral of preemptive expectations which would lead

7. Raymond Aron, *The Great Debate: Theories of Nuclear Strategy,* trans. Ernst Pavel (Doubleday, 1965), pp. 61–62.

8. Fitzroy Maclean, "Nuclear Deterrence and Conventional Forces," *Brassey's Annual 1970* (Praeger, 1970), pp. 4–5.

to [strategic war]."[9] At a minimum, therefore, U.S. tactical nuclear strategy must take into consideration, as Secretary Schlesinger has already, the fact that while "it is essential to theorize about the nature of tactical nuclear warfare, we must acknowledge that as a practical matter, the initiation of a nuclear engagement would involve many uncertainties. Acceptable boundaries on such a conflict would be extremely difficult to establish."[10]

The Incompatibility of Weaponry and Doctrine

The most prominent weakness of U.S. tactical nuclear posture in Europe is the incompatibility of the current TNW deployment with existing doctrinal prescriptions for its use. As questionable as the efficaciousness of those prescriptions may be in the context of a war in Europe, there is little doubt that the number of tactical nuclear warheads maintained in the European area exceeds that required for the kind of selective response preferred by U.S. and NATO planners. The same may be said of the size of many U.S. warheads, whose use in Europe would risk inflicting a level of collateral damage at variance with doctrinal objectives. Moreover, the vulnerability of many U.S. systems to preemptive strike or to early capture is incongruent with the kind of stable tactical nuclear deterrent sought by the Atlantic Alliance. Finally, present measures for the command and control of TNW are not adequate insurance against unauthorized use, since in wartime they would not preclude access to many warheads on the part of local U.S. commanders likely to come under direct fire.

A Surfeit of Warheads

Aside from the difficulties inherent in insuring the physical safety and control of over 7,000 nuclear warheads, a deployment of such magnitude appears "dangerously excessive" for the requirements of present NATO strategy.[11] Even assuming the availability of a substantial number

9. Morton H. Halperin, *Limited War in the Nuclear Age* (John Wiley and Sons, 1963), p. 64.

10. *Annual Defense Department Report, FY 1975*, p. 82.

11. Paul C. Warnke, Statement before the Subcommittee on U.S. Security Agreements and Commitments Abroad of the Senate Foreign Relations Committee (March 14, 1974; processed), p. 18.

of worthwhile military targets, a NATO nuclear strike that employed only a small fraction of its present arsenal—say, 1,000 warheads— would hardly be selective (to say nothing of demonstrative) since it could not avoid wreaking widespread collateral damage over vast areas, including in all probability sizable portions of West Germany. A posture geared to truly discriminating uses of TNW most likely could be served with warheads of both battlefield and theater caliber numbering in the several hundreds rather than thousands. An inventory of this size for European contingencies has been proposed by numerous analysts, among them Paul Warnke and Alain C. Enthoven.[12]

Extravagant Yields

The destructiveness of many U.S. TNW also surpasses the degree sufficient for discrete use at either the battlefield or theater level, although this excess of kilotonage is moderated somewhat by the selectable yields of some warheads. The conclusion that the present inventory represents a "stockpile of overly high-yield tactical nuclear weapons" ill suited for the type of conflict envisaged by U.S. planners[13] is shared by a majority of analysts, including those who support a predominately nuclear defense of Western Europe.[14]

It is difficult to imagine, for example, the possible battlefield uses of an 80- or 100-kiloton warhead (six or eight times the yield of the Hiroshima bomb), although warheads selectable to this yield are carried by the *Lance,* the most recent addition to the U.S. deployment of battlefield surface-to-surface missiles. Equally inconceivable, if not more so, are theater military targets, even in Eastern Europe, that would warrant the employment of the 400 to 1,000 kiloton (one megaton) warheads deliverable, respectively, by a number of *Pershing* missiles and some tactical aircraft. There is virtually no probable military staging area or installation in East Germany, Poland, or Czechoslovakia where TNW of this magnitude could be detonated without causing immense collateral

---

12. Ibid., p. 13, and Enthoven, Statement on U.S. Military Forces in Europe before the Senate Committee on Foreign Relations (March 14, 1974; processed), p. 15.

13. Phillip A. Karber, "Nuclear Weapons and 'Flexible Response,'" *Orbis,* vol. 14 (Summer 1970), p. 292.

14. See, for example, Robert M. Lawrence, "On Tactical Nuclear War: Part II," *Revue Militaire Générale* (February 1971), and R. C. Richardson, "Can NATO Fashion a New Strategy?" *Orbis,* vol. 17 (Summer 1973).

damage.[15] Indeed, the use of such weapons by NATO would necessarily reflect a substantial and highly escalatory departure from any pretense of restrained nuclear combat.

Unnecessary Vulnerability

The vulnerability of many European-deployed U.S. TNW either to a preemptive strike or to capture has long been a serious concern of the Atlantic Alliance. This concern is justified because large, exposed weapon systems and installations work to destabilize deterrence by presenting the enemy lucrative and easily destroyable targets that might encourage a surprise attack.

Most of NATO's nuclear-capable tactical aircraft in Europe are particularly vulnerable to preemption because they are deployed on a relatively small number of operational airfields in a geographic area which, compared to the vast expanses of Eastern Europe and European Russia, is decidedly constrained. Past and present NATO programs aimed at increasing the protection of individual aircraft by revetments and other measures are valuable hedges against conventional attack but are not likely to reduce the vulnerability of both aircraft and airfields to the blast and thermal effects of nuclear strikes. Only by the dispersion of planes among a much larger number of airfields might present vulnerability to nuclear preemption be reduced.

The physical vulnerability of NATO's European-deployed tactical aircraft to a surprise nuclear strike must be weighed, however, against other factors that serve to discourage such a Soviet attack. First, a Soviet strike "out of the blue" certainly represents the worst-case scenario, since in all likelihood NATO would receive political if not military warning time before the event. If NATO acted promptly following such warning, some dispersion of planes to bases that are not currently operational would be possible within two or three weeks. Second, a preemptive Soviet nuclear strike of the magnitude necessary to deprive NATO's forward-deployed air forces of an effective tactical nuclear second-strike capacity would run an extremely grave risk of sparking a major nuclear conflict perhaps involving the use of strategic weapons by the United States. Third, a Soviet attack directed against only European targets

15. Dissatisfaction with the excessive yields of the *Pershing* has led the U.S. Army to request funds in the fiscal year 1975 defense budget for the development of a *Pershing II* warhead of about one kiloton possessing a much more accurate guidance system (*Washington Post,* Jan. 24, 1974).

would leave intact the potential for a tactical nuclear riposte deliverable by the hundreds of nuclear-capable tactical aircraft based in the United States. These aircraft, however, would have to be transferred to European airfields before launching; thus the number that actually could be employed would be contingent upon how many European airfields remained operational following the outbreak of hostilities.

Nuclear-capable artillery constitutes another category of notably vulnerable TNW. Although the number, mobility, and relatively small size of NATO's 155-mm and 8-inch howitzers render the deployment comparatively immune from effective preemption, these artillery pieces are peculiarly vulnerable to capture in wartime. Their very limited ranges necessitate their combat employment in extremely close proximity to engaged enemy forces. This fact, coupled with the presumption of the Pact as the attacker, strongly suggests that many of the guns would be overrun in the early stages of fighting. An attack following distribution of nuclear projectiles to selected NATO batteries deployed well forward raises the specter of losing both guns and warheads to the enemy. Captured intact, these systems would confer upon Soviet forces certain battlefield tactical nuclear capabilities that they do not now possess.

Temptations of Unauthorized Use

Present arrangements and procedures designed to protect U.S. nuclear weapons and to prevent their unauthorized use in peacetime appear adequate, although continuing care must be exercised in screening personnel who are granted access to these weapons.[16] The maintenance of proper command and control over nuclear weapons, particularly tactical systems, promises to be infinitely more difficult in time of war. Formidable hedges against possible misuse are apparent in the strict and redundant procedures regulating air-delivered weapons and in the assignment of all U.S. tactical surface-to-surface missiles in Europe to the USAREUR Missile Forces, a separate command directly responsible to the President via SACEUR. This arrangement, unless it were modified

16. In 1972 and the first three months of 1973, a total of no fewer than 3,647 U.S. military and civilian employees with access to nuclear weapons were removed from their jobs "because of drug abuse, mental illness, alcoholism or disciplinary problems." According to General Andrew J. Goodpaster, Supreme Allied Commander in Europe (SACEUR), from 1971 to mid-1973 1,247 "nuclear specialists" within the North Atlantic Treaty Organization were "removed under a program designed to identify those who might be subject to blackmail or irrational behavior" (*Washington Post,* Jan. 27, 1974).

by the President, precludes direct access to tactical nuclear SSM by local U.S. commanders even at the division or corps level and thus greatly simplifies command and control.

The same cannot be said, however, of NATO's nuclear-capable artillery, most of which is organic to both U.S. and allied divisions. Once nuclear warheads have been distributed to designated batteries, they become physically accessible to local commanders, many of whom in the midst of combat would probably be subjected to severe pressures to make unauthorized use of these weapons or at least to employ them in a manner beyond whatever authorization was granted. The likelihood that many of these batteries would be engaged in close combat with the enemy has been noted, as has the probability that some units to which the batteries are assigned would be either overrun or encircled in the early phases of the war. Is it not reasonable to assume that a local commander, threatened with the destruction or capture of his entire command and perhaps denied effective communication with higher headquarters, would be sorely tempted to employ the nuclear weapons at his disposal prematurely or without regard to presidential directive? This possibility raises the issue of whether the presumed battlefield utility of nuclear-capable artillery is outweighed by the difficulty of controlling its use. Indeed, it was precisely problems of command and control as well as inherent vulnerability to capture that led the United States in the 1960s to retire from its TNW inventory in Europe the *Davy Crockett,* a short-range, jeep-mounted nuclear recoilless rifle.[17]

17. Lloyd Norman, "The Reluctant Dragon: NATO's Fears and the Need for New Nuclear Weapons," *Army,* vol. 24 (February 1974), p. 19; Lawrence Martin, *Arms and Strategy: The World Power Structure Today* (David McKay, 1973), p. 135; and "Report on Tactical Nuclear Weapons," a research paper prepared by the office of Senator Gaylord Nelson for consideration by the Military Spending Committee of Members of *Congress for Peace Through Law* (July 16, 1971), pp. 11–12.

CHAPTER SEVEN

ALTERNATIVE POSTURES

Analysis of the weaknesses of present U.S. tactical nuclear posture in Europe suggests a variety of alternatives, some of which are investigated in this chapter. Their probable impact on deterrence, defense, and the overall stability of the military balance in Europe is assessed, and, where possible, the political and budgetary implications of each alternative are identified. The alternatives presented here by no means exhaust the possibilities of transforming U.S. tactical nuclear posture on the continent; indeed, proposals other than the ones discussed in this study are plentiful throughout the literature.[1] Moreover, whether the measures contained in the various alternatives should be undertaken unilaterally by the U.S. and its allies or be made contingent upon some kind of quid pro quo on the part of the Soviet Union is a question that goes beyond the scope of this study.

Four alternatives are considered. The first envisages merely a reduction in the number of U.S. TNW and is designed to simplify command and control and to decrease the instability inherent in what many observers believe is an excessive deployment. Alternative 2 has similar aims but contemplates the elimination of particularly vulnerable TNW as well as measures to reduce the vulnerability of remaining systems. A credible warfighting capability is the objective of Alternative 3, which calls for the replacement of most currently deployed TNW by new, miniaturized nuclear weapons, whose very limited destructive effects proponents claim would minimize collateral damage and preclude escalation to a wider nuclear war. Alternative 4 envisages a U.S. renunciation of a tactical nuclear defense of Western Europe, followed by the re-

1. See, for example, Wolfgang Heisenberg, *The Alliance and Europe: Part I: Crisis Stability in Europe and Theatre Nuclear Weapons*, Adelphi Papers, 96 (London: International Institute for Strategic Studies, 1973), and Morton A. Kaplan, *NATO and Dissuasion* (University of Chicago, 1974).

moval of all U.S. TNW from the continent. This alternative represents the extreme view that the United States should not deploy any non-strategic weapon systems whose use, it is argued, would automatically trigger a strategic holocaust.

Alternative 1: A Smaller Deployment

Dissatisfaction with the size of the U.S. tactical nuclear deployment in the European area is widespread, and many observers have called for reductions in the number of systems on the continent. Indeed, Secretary of Defense James R. Schlesinger has stated publicly that the deployment's present size is "not immutable" and could be reduced "under certain circumstances";[2] according to one report, he "is planning on reducing the sizable stockpile of nuclear weapons in Europe as well as cutting back on the number of atomic-armed missiles and planes kept on [Quick Reaction] alert."[3]

A major rationale for reduction, discussed in Chapter 6, is that the current deployment "is excessively redundant"[4] for either deterrence or defense, even if a credible warfighting role for TNW is assumed. Additional and perhaps more important arguments are that the magnitude of the present stockpile complicates problems of command and control and ties down substantial manpower and equipment (particularly aircraft) that otherwise could be employed to bolster conventional defense.

It is the author's judgment that the grounds for reduction are compelling, although the number of TNW that could be eliminated from the European deployment without disturbing NATO's capacity to deter or to wage a tactical nuclear war is purely speculative. Enthoven has suggested that 1,000 TNW (divided between SSM and artillery shells) would be sufficient for both purposes,[5] while former Assistant Secretary of Defense Paul C. Warnke has testified that the "deterrent purpose of

2. Dan Morgan, "Nuclear Force in Europe Held Open to Cutting," *Washington Post,* April 4, 1974.

3. John W. Finney, "Schlesinger Set to Cut A-Arms," *New York Times,* April 25, 1974.

4. Dennis M. Gormley, "NATO's Tactical Nuclear Option: Past, Present and Future," *Military Review,* vol. 53 (September 1973), p. 14.

5. A Statement by Alain C. Enthoven on U.S. Military Forces in Europe before the Senate Committee on Foreign Relations (March 14, 1974; processed), p. 15.

tactical [nuclear] weapons could abundantly be served by the maintenance of a few hundred at most."[6]

Either of these proposals, if carried out, would involve the removal of at least 6,000 U.S. TNW from Europe, which in turn could result in either substantial budgetary savings or the enhancement of NATO's conventional deterrent. Assuming that an average of five troops are presently assigned to operate, maintain, and protect each weapon deployed (see discussion of costs in Chapter 5), the number of personnel directly affected by a reduction of 6,000 TNW on the continent would be about 30,000. This figure does not include personnel involved in supporting U.S. "tactical nuclear" troops. If 30,000 spaces were eliminated entirely from the force structure, the annual savings in Military Personnel costs alone could amount to $321 million in fiscal 1975 dollars;[7] if, however, they were kept in the structure and retained in Europe they would represent the addition to NATO's conventional deterrent of the equivalent of almost a full U.S. division and its initial supporting units.[8]

The question of what to do with manpower freed by TNW reductions in Europe is a crucial one. To cut from the force structure 30,000 U.S. troops now stationed in Europe would probably be interpreted in many European capitals—both East and West—as a weakening of U.S. willingness to defend its continental allies. If undertaken unilaterally, a troop reduction of such magnitude would also seriously erode the U.S. bargaining position at the MBFR talks in Vienna. On the other hand, a decision to retain the 30,000 troops in Europe to bolster NATO's conventional deterrent would put the European members of the alliance on notice that the United States in an era of strategic parity is more than ever committed to a strategy of response that is truly flexible. Indeed, the transfer of so many U.S. troops from nuclear to nonnuclear functions might stimulate other NATO members to increase their own contributions to conventional defense.

6. Paul C. Warnke, Statement before the Subcommittee on U.S. Security Agreements and Commitments Abroad of the Senate Foreign Relations Committee (March 14, 1974; processed), p. 13.

7. Assuming a reduction of 26,000 U.S. Army and 4,000 U.S. Air Force personnel representing, respectively, a fiscal 1975 per capita Military Personnel expenditure of $10,500 and $12,000 (26,000 $\times$ $10,500 + 4,000 $\times$ $12,100 = $321,000,000).

8. A U.S. division and its Initial Supporting Increment (the support personnel required to sustain the division for up to 60 days in combat) numbers about 32,000 men. The U.S. Army, Europe (USAREUR) presently contains four and one-third divisions and about 199,000 men.

Proposals for sizable reductions in U.S. TNW in Europe encounter objections based primarily on political grounds. Many observers, although convinced that a smaller deployment would not adversely affect deterrence, defense, or the present overall military balance on the continent, believe nevertheless that any major cut would be highly detrimental to NATO's political fabric because it would be viewed—however mistakenly—by West Europeans as a "decoupling" of the U.S. strategic deterrent from Europe's defense. It is true that America's European allies, especially the West Germans, do attach great importance to the presence of large numbers of deployed U.S. TNW as not only the most visible link to the U.S. deterrent but also a symbol of the broader American commitment to allied defense.[9] As one observer has concluded,

If one were able to ignore the history of the past fifteen or twenty years, I believe that it would have been possible to maintain the credibility of the American guarantee to Germany . . . without the stationing of nuclear weapons in Europe. However . . . the Germans have become used to the presence of American nuclear weapons in Europe and they have come to see them as a part of the deterrent making it more credible that the United States would ultimately use strategic weapons. For this reason I do not believe that the United States should contemplate the withdrawal of all its nuclear weapons from Europe. I do believe, however, that it should be possible to make a substantial reduction. . . .[10]

Stanley Hoffmann has voiced similar conclusions:

My argument is not that we should under no circumstances reduce . . . the tactical nuclear stockpile—but that we have to be very careful about the context and the deal . . .

[T]he removal of U.S. troops would still leave U.S. nuclear forces alongside the European armies, whereas the existence of European forces without the tactical link to the U.S. strategic deterrent would encourage the neutralism of Europeans and the "decoupling" proclivities of Americans.[11]

Indeed, at least one prominent European commentator has urged that "any weakening in the credibility of the strategic deterrent or in the level of American troops should be met by strengthening the essential link—[U.S.] theater nuclear weapons—rather than weakening it."[12]

---

9. A concise review of West German attitudes toward tactical nuclear weapons may be found in Charles H. Davidson, "Tactical Nuclear Defense: The West German View," *Parameters* (1974, No. 1), pp. 47–57.

10. Morton H. Halperin, Statement before the Subcommittee on United States Security Agreements and Commitments Abroad of the Senate Foreign Relations Committee (March 7, 1974; processed), pp. 12–13.

11. Stanley Hoffmann, in ibid., p. 13.

12. Pierre Hassner, "A NATO Dissuasion Strategy: A French View," in Kaplan, *NATO and Dissuasion*, p. 101.

In sum, although a reduction of U.S. TNW is warranted, it must be undertaken in a manner that preserves European confidence in the United States. This suggests (1) that the postreduction deployment still possess enough visibility to satisfy the European desire for a credible tactical link to the U.S. strategic deterrent, and (2) that the process of reduction be accompanied at every stage by consultation among the allies.

Alternative 2: A Smaller and Less Vulnerable Deployment

Alternative 1 calls for a simple reduction in the number of U.S. TNW deployed in Europe. Alternative 2 also envisages a smaller deployment but one composed of TNW that are less exposed to preemption or to capture than is now the case. This objective would be achieved mainly through selective elimination from the force of weapons that are particularly vulnerable, and measures to reduce the vulnerability of remaining systems.

Candidates for partial or complete elimination would include nuclear artillery shells and bombs, whose delivery systems' comparative vulnerability to surprise attack or to enemy seizure was discussed in Chapter 6. Nuclear-capable aircraft, which would not be eliminated, would be dispersed among a larger number of bases, and relatively immobile ground-launched TNW would be replaced by more nimble systems, a development already under way with the deployment of the *Lance* and the retirement of the *Sergeant* and *Honest John*. The resulting deployment would be one dominated by ground-launched surface-to-surface missiles, supplemented by some tactical aircraft and perhaps a few howitzers designated for nuclear employment. To reduce the prospect of unauthorized use, all howitzers allocated for nuclear use would be placed under the direct command and control of USAREUR Missile Forces.

Although smaller and less reliant on air-delivered ordnance, Alternative 2's advantages over the present deployment are obvious: simplified command and control, reduced prospects for unauthorized use, less manpower and aircraft diverted from conventional defense, and diminished vulnerability to preemption—most of which make for a more stable tactical nuclear deterrent. Indeed, the author believes the effect, if any, that the proposed eliminations might have on tactical nuclear capabilities would be more than offset by the new deployment's greater invulnerability.

Another measure that might be subsumed under Alternative 2 is the termination of Quick Reaction Alert, which many analysts believe increases the possibility of a nuclear exchange because systems kept on QRA constitute a standing *invitation* to preemption.[13] A legacy of the massive retaliation era, the maintenance in a constant state of readiness of certain nuclear-loaded aircraft and missiles poised to deliver nuclear strikes against theater *and* strategic targets appears decidedly out of step with the desire for true flexibility that characterizes present NATO strategy. The same can be said of atomic demolition munitions, which by their very nature would, once prechambered, impose a rigidity on tactical planning and operations that could adversely affect the forward defense of Western Europe. Moreover, the contribution to overall deployed tactical nuclear capabilities made by the TNW that are maintained on QRA is marginal. The termination of QRA certainly would not weaken the U.S. strategic deterrent, the bulk of which is deployed outside the European area; if anything, it would reduce the likelihood of the deterrent's ever being used by increasing the number of aircraft available for conventional defense. The proposition that Quick Reaction Alert's destabilizing influence on the military balance in Europe outweighs whatever minor tactical warfighting advantages it may confer on NATO apparently has been accepted by Secretary Schlesinger, who is reportedly planning to reduce the number of systems kept on QRA.[14]

Objections to Alternative 2 are similar to those to Alternative 1. Any major reduction of U.S. TNW on the continent, even though its outcome in this case would be a more secure and less redundant deployment, would, it is argued, be interpreted by many Western Europeans as a weakening of the U.S. commitment to their defense. Particular importance is attached to Quick Reaction Alert: of all U.S. TNW in Europe, those maintained on QRA—because many are semistrategic and postured to deliver a near-instantaneous riposte to aggression—constitute the most visible connection to the U.S. strategic deterrent. Indeed, although removal of nuclear artillery shells and ADM would be unlikely to stimulate much allied opposition,[15] strong resistance may

13. See, for example, Walter Pincus, "Nukes Nobody Needs," *New Republic,* vol. 170 (April 20, 1974), and W. S. Bennett, R. R. Sandoval, and R. G. Shreffler, "A Credible Nuclear-Emphasis Defense for NATO," *Orbis,* vol. 17 (Summer 1973).

14. Finney, "Schlesinger Set to Cut A-Arms."

15. Europeans "have resisted . . . vigorously the efforts of the United States to put into place nuclear weapons which suggested the possibility of fighting a limited nuclear war" (Halperin, Statement Before the Senate Foreign Relations Subcommittee, p. 10).

be expected to any proposal that would tamper with what one German observer has characterized as "the necessary link between conventional warfare and the use of strategic nuclear arms."[16]

Thus, the realization of Alternative 2, like Alternative 1, should be contingent upon preliminary interallied consultation and agreement. This imposes upon the United States the task of convincing its NATO partners that the measures proposed in Alternative 2 would erode neither the U.S. commitment to Europe's defense nor, more specifically, U.S. willingness to undertake a nuclear response to aggression should circumstances require it—a task that would be facilitated if U.S. troops released from tactical nuclear functions were retained on the continent.

The budgetary consequences of Alternative 2 are difficult to estimate because they would depend on a number of factors: the number and types of TNW removed from the inventory; whether or not the manpower associated with those TNW were retained in the force structure; the degree to which deployed nuclear-capable tactical aircraft were dispersed; and whether Quick Reaction Alert were terminated or, as apparently envisaged by Secretary Schlesinger, merely contracted. If all personnel affected by the reduction of TNW were retained and if QRA were left undisturbed,[17] little net savings could be expected. If, on the other hand, QRA were dropped entirely and manpower associated with eliminated TNW were also cut from the force structure, the resulting savings probably would more than offset the costs of aircraft dispersal.

Alternative 3: A Warfighting Deployment

Although resolving many problems related to vulnerability and to command and control, neither Alternative 1 nor Alternative 2 addresses what many critics believe is the principal weakness of U.S. tactical nuclear posture in Europe; namely, that present yields are too large to permit their actual use without risking the wholesale destruction of the very Europe that NATO was founded to protect. Simply reducing the number of TNW on the continent, it is argued, would still leave in place a panoply of weapons of such destructiveness that their employment

16. Wolfgang Wagner, "A NATO Dissuasion Strategy: A German View," in Kaplan, *NATO and Dissuasion*, p. 138.
17. Although reliable figures are not available, the annual cost of maintaining the present number of U.S. systems on QRA is estimated by the author to be in the tens of millions of dollars.

would not only preclude a meaningful defense of Western Europe but also threaten rapid escalation even to strategic nuclear war. In sum, "given NATO's current [tactical nuclear] capabilities, crossing the nuclear threshold would be so disastrous as to lose all credibility as a rational option."[18]

The solution, treated here as a separate alternative although it is certainly not incompatible with Alternatives 1 or 2, lies in reducing yields of existing weapons and ultimately in the development and deployment of a new family of TNW whose effects would more resemble large conventional munitions than existing nuclear ordnance. It is claimed that the limited destructiveness of miniaturized TNW would confer upon NATO a true nuclear warfighting capability that would at the same time be "clearly not escalatory."[19] Therefore they could and should be used along with conventional arms from the very start of hostilities, thus permitting NATO to avoid the political agony of crossing the atomic threshold, which in the context of present high-yield TNW is admittedly fraught with danger. Indeed, some proponents of miniaturization view the new weapons as a substitute for rather than a supplement to conventional defense.

Supporters of "mini-nukes" include atomic scientists, civilian defense analysts, and a number of high-ranking military leaders and Department of Defense officials. Indeed, although the technology of miniaturization is still largely in the research and development stage, for the past several years pressures within the U.S. military establishment for procurement of mini-nukes have been strong enough to suggest that miniaturization was under earnest consideration by the Nixon administration and continues to be under the Ford administration.[20] While there are no indications of an official shift away from flexible response toward a predominantly nuclear defense of Europe, Secretary Schlesinger has publicly referred to the "serious possibilities of replacing the existing [tactical nuclear] stockpile with nuclear weapons and systems more

18. Phillip A. Karber, "Nuclear Weapons and 'Flexible Response,'" *Orbis,* vol. 14 (Summer 1970), p. 291.

19. R. G. Shreffler and W. S. Bennett, "Tactical Nuclear Warfare" (Los Alamos Scientific Laboratory of the University of California, 1970; processed), p. 5.

20. In May 1974, Joseph Martin, the U.S. ambassador to the Geneva Disarmament Conference, publicly stated "categorically that the U.S. Government has no intention whatever to treat such tactical systems as interchangeable with conventional arms"; however, he went on to say that his policy would not preclude the United States from undertaking "qualitative" improvements in present types of TNW, including reducing yields and improving accuracy of delivery vehicles (Michael Getler, "U.S. Offers 'Mini-Nuke' Assurance," *Washington Post,* May 24, 1974).

appropriate" to a variety of aims, including those of "denying the enemy his military objectives without excessive collateral damage," and "providing for selective, carefully-controlled employment options."[21] Army Chief of Staff Creighton W. Abrams, appearing before the House Armed Services Committee in 1974, testified: "We need, as a matter of urgent priority, an improved family of tactical nuclear artillery weapons to provide the field commander the precise ability to inflict damage on his enemy with greatly decreased collateral damage to non-military targets."[22] Echoing these sentiments, General Andrew J. Goodpaster, the present NATO SACEUR, has said that "new weapons of lower yields and of greater accuracy could increase military effectiveness, while reducing possible collateral damage, thereby increasing their utility as well as the acceptability in NATO planning for employment in the NATO countries and the adjacent areas in which they would most likely be used."[23]

Miniaturization of TNW is certainly well within the technological reach of the United States and could be achieved in two ways. First, yields of fission-reaction warheads (all present U.S. TNW are fission devices) could be cut to the point where their blast and thermal effects would be equivalent to less than 100 tons of TNT (0.1 kiloton). Residual radiation also could be reduced although not curtailed altogether. A second approach, albeit a much more difficult and costly one, would be to develop either a low-yield fusion ("neutron") bomb, whose energy would be released primarily in the form of prompt radiation, or a pure fusion weapon,[24] which would produce virtually "no residual radioactivity,"[25] thus avoiding much of the political stigma attached to the use of nuclear weapons. The ability to minimize collateral damage would be further enhanced if, as has been proposed, miniaturized warheads were carried by precision-guided delivery systems such as "smart" bombs; the combination of reduced radii of destruction and greater

21. Statement by Secretary of Defense James R. Schlesinger before the Subcommittees on U.S. Security Agreements and Commitments Abroad and Arms Control, International Law and Organization of the Senate Foreign Relations Committee (April 4, 1974; processed), pp. 3, 4.

22. Statement by General Creighton W. Abrams before the House Committee on Armed Services (Feb. 14, 1974; processed), p. 22.

23. John W. Finney, "Small Atomic Arms are Urged for NATO," *New York Times,* Jan. 27, 1974.

24. Although many U.S. strategic weapons are fusion devices, they are not "pure" because under present technology the heat necessary to initiate a fusion reaction can be generated only by a prior fission reaction.

25. Robert M. Lawrence, "On Tactical Nuclear War: Part II," *Revue Militaire Générale* (February 1971), p. 242.

delivery accuracy strongly implies a capacity for truly discriminate use of TNW.

The superior *battlefield* utility of mini-nukes over the present relatively high-yield TNW is obvious. Moreover, a NATO reliant first and foremost on such weapons rather than conventional arms for the defense of Western Europe would be spared the cost of maintaining the massive logistics infrastructure, huge ammunition stockpiles, and, it is claimed, much of the manpower now necessary to muster a credible nonnuclear deterrent;[26] a single nuclear projectile equivalent to 50 tons of TNT is far more manageable than 1,000 conventional projectiles of 100 pounds each.

The arguments against miniaturization, however, are perhaps more important. The first addresses the contention, widely shared among miniaturization supporters, that "a strong Soviet conventional attack . . . can be held in check only by the instantaneous use of tactical nuclear weapons."[27] Acceptance of this proposition *would* dictate the substitution of a tactical nuclear for a conventional defense, which in turn would require dropping the present strategy of flexible response in favor of a more rigid doctrine tailored to the use of nuclear weapons as the initial and primary means of countering aggression. But, as discussed in Chapter 3, the proposition that Europe is conventionally indefensible is far from self-evident, suggesting that TNW of whatever type should continue to be envisaged as a supplement to, not a substitute for, conventional defense. Indeed, whether Europe is defensible without resort to nuclear weapons has been the subject of extensive debate on both sides of the Atlantic ever since the Kennedy administration's adoption of flexible response. In this regard, it is worth noting that recent Department of Defense studies have convinced Secretary Schlesinger that "there is an approximate balance between the immediately available [conventional] forces of NATO and the Warsaw Pact in the Center Region."[28]

A second major argument against miniaturization is that the deployment of mini-nukes, even as a supplement to conventional defense, would make nuclear conflict more likely by lowering the nuclear threshold to the point where a conventional and a nuclear response could

26. The question of whether, in the context of the European military balance, manpower can be effectively traded for TNW is treated in Chapter 3.

27. Stephen T. Possony, "NATO's Defense Posture," *Ordnance*, vol. 14 (July–August 1969), p. 42.

28. *Annual Defense Department Report, FY 1975*, p. 88.

become indistinguishable. The very "usability" of the weapons, particularly if they were governed by a doctrine of immediate employment, would obliterate the political constraints on crossing the threshold.

Moreover, there arises the obvious question, raised as early as 1966 by Raymond Aron: "What is the use of violating the 'atomic taboo' if one does not use weapons more powerful than conventional weapons?"[29] Although in terms of sheer destructive power mini-nukes undoubtedly would be superior to present nonnuclear weapon systems, Aron's query is increasingly apropos in light of the revolutionary technological developments now taking place in the West in conventional mine warfare, "smart" bombs and artillery, and precision-guided rockets and missiles, as well as those that are expected in the field of laser-kill weapons systems—all of which would raise the threshold by greatly strengthening NATO's ability to thwart invasion without resort to nuclear arms.[30]

Third, there is scant evidence to support the assertion that mini-nukes, because of their limited destructiveness, could be employed with little risk of escalation. This would presume Soviet acceptance of them not as nuclear devices but simply as improved conventional ordnance. Aside from the fact that weight of informed opinion still holds that "the use of non-atomic explosives" is "the best protection against escalation,"[31] Soviet military doctrine, as analyzed in Chapter 5, leaves little room for

29. Raymond Aron, *Peace and War: A Theory of International Relations,* trans. Richard Howard and Annette Baker Fox (Doubleday, 1966), p. 495.

30. For a discussion of these and other developments in conventional weapons technology, see Trevor Cliffe, *Military Technology and the European Balance,* Adelphi Papers, 89 (London: International Institute for Strategic Studies, 1972); Stefan Geisenheyner, "A Defensive Weapons Mix for Europe," *Survival,* vol. 13 (September 1971); John T. Burke, " 'Smart' Weapons: A Coming Revolution in Tactics," *Army,* vol. 23 (February 1973); and Kenneth Hunt, *The Alliance and Europe: Part II: Defense with Fewer Men* (London: International Institute for Strategic Studies, 1973).

31. "The truth of this proposition is based on psychological probability. Rightly or wrongly, men, at all ranges of the social scale, establish a radical discrimination between conventional weapons and atomic weapons. So long as only the first are in action, opinion—that of the leaders of governments as well as of the governed—correctly assumes that the desire for moderation exists on both sides. This discrimination between the two types of weapons remains valid despite today's reestablished continuity between chemical explosives and atomic explosives (the least powerful of the latter category being perhaps less powerful than the most powerful of the former). The reason this discrimination remains rational is that it is the simplest one that enemies can simultaneously acknowledge without needing communication or explicit agreement" (Aron, *Peace and War,* pp. 493–94).

doubt that even the smallest TNW "would be regarded . . . by Soviet forces" as "*not* different in kind" from other nuclear weapons.[32] In other words,

The main problem . . . is whether small-yield and "clean" tactical nuclear weapons can provide a more promising means of deterrence. . . . For purposes of military defense it is evident that more efficient weapons will also offer greater military advantages, initially at least. But . . . possible Soviet reactions must be taken into account in the assessment. The use of "small and clean" nuclear warheads by NATO is likely to be countered by the Warsaw Pact deploying its nuclear weapons, which, being less technologically advanced and less accurate will cause a much higher degree of destruction and radioactive fall-out. The hope that the Soviet side will not classify the "mini-nukes" as nuclear weapons . . . seems unfounded; the changeover from conventional into nuclear warfare has been regarded for too long as a major qualitative break ("fire-break") to be dismissed as a mere technicality.[33]

And in fact the Soviets so far have derided proposals to arm NATO forces with mini-nukes, claiming that the use of any nuclear weapons in a European conflict would probably result in expansion of hostilities into general nuclear war.[34]

A fourth argument against the deployment of mini-nukes is that it would probably be unacceptable to many Western European governments, particularly the Federal Republic of Germany. As noted above, Western European opinion has traditionally opposed the U.S. deployment of TNW that raised the prospect of fighting a nuclear war that did not engage—or at least ominously threaten to engage—the U.S. strategic deterrent. Resistance would almost certainly be stronger to "the development of a capability which suggested the United States was attempting to build a fire break between small tactical nuclear weapons and large [ones]."[35]

Finally, there is the matter of cost. Unlike the other alternatives investigated in this chapter, the realization of Alternative 3 would involve major net budgetary outlays.[36] Although the cost of developing and pro-

32. Hunt, *The Alliance and Europe, Part II*, p. 18.

33. Heisenberg, *The Alliance and Europe, Part I*, p. 11.

34. Leon Gouré, Foy D. Kohler, and Mose L. Harvey, *The Role of Nuclear Forces in Current Soviet Strategy* (University of Miami Press, 1974), p. 129.

35. Halperin, Statement before the Senate Foreign Relations Subcommittee, p. 10.

36. A large portion—perhaps as much as 30 percent—of the cost of Alternative 3 would be recoverable since nuclear materials such as oralloy and enriched uranium in warheads designated for replacement by mini-nukes could be reworked and resold for use by nonmilitary consumers of nuclear energy. Recoverable costs would, of course, be an aspect of any proposal, such as Alternatives 1 and 2, to reduce the present number of TNW in the U.S. inventory.

cessing a family of new, miniaturized TNW does not lend itself to accurate estimation at the present time, there is little doubt that it would be in the order of hundreds of millions, if not billions, of fiscal 1975 dollars. For example, Deputy Assistant Secretary of Defense William Beecher has cited an estimate of $400 million annually over a period of several years.[37] This projection appears somewhat conservative in light of the AEC's unsuccessful fiscal 1974 budget request for $904 million to miniaturize just nuclear artillery shells. Indeed, research and development costs alone related to smaller nuclear warheads exceeded $35 million in the fiscal 1975 budget.[38]

Alternative 4: No Deployment

Alternative 4 calls for a U.S. renunciation of the possibility of a tactical nuclear defense of Europe and the removal of all deployed U.S. TNW. The reasoning behind this alternative is that the contribution made by deployed TNW to overall deterrence of aggression is at best marginal, and in any event is clearly outweighed by the escalation to strategic war that would, it is argued, inevitably follow the actual use of TNW.[39] The corollary of this premise is that Europe's defense must be entrusted exclusively to conventional forces.

As has been shown, the author accepts neither the proposition of automatic escalation to total war nor the claim that TNW are valueless as a deterrent. It is his opinion that the presence of U.S. nuclear weapons in Europe—however difficult it is to envisage their actual use—does impose upon Soviet military planners a high degree of tactical uncer-

37. William Beecher, " 'Clean' Tactical Nuclear Weapons for Europe: Over the Threshold," *Army*, vol. 22 (July 1972), p. 20.

38. Including, for the AEC, $27 million for "advanced research, development and testing for new technology related to tactical systems"; and for the Army, $4.75 million "for studies and development of ballistic shapes, fusing, and other hardware related to new nuclear artillery warheads," and an additional $3.75 million pertaining to missiles. *Fiscal Year 1975 Authorization for Military Procurement, Research and Development, and Active Duty, Selected Reserve and Civilian Personnel Strengths, Part I: Authorization,* Hearings before the Senate Committee on Armed Services, 93 Cong. 2 sess. (1974), p. 309.

39. This view was quite prevalent within the Kennedy administration. For example, Deputy Secretary of Defense Roswell Gilpatric publicly asserted that "I, for one, have never believed in a so-called limited nuclear war. I just don't know how you build a limit into it once you start using any kind of nuclear bang" (quoted in Henry Kissinger, "NATO's Nuclear Dilemma," *The Reporter* [March 28, 1963], p. 24). See also President Kennedy's statement cited in note 12, p. 14, above.

tainty. Moreover, as discussed in Chapter 5, current Soviet nuclear doctrine is notably ambiguous on the relationship of theater to strategic nuclear conflict.

The greatest weakness of Alternative 4, however, is that it ignores the tremendous political significance of deployed U.S. TNW to our European allies. Governments that would tend to interpret the mere reduction of U.S. TNW on the continent as an erosion of the American commitment to defend Europe would be likely to view the complete withdrawal of those weapons as signaling the termination of that commitment. The result could well be the disintegration of an already politically battered NATO and perhaps even the "Finlandization" of Western Europe itself.

In Conclusion

An alternative to the present U.S. tactical nuclear posture in Europe, a posture now ill suited for credible deterrence or defense, is clearly in order. Both the number and the destructive power of U.S. TNW on the continent are excessive for either purpose, and the deployment is needlessly vulnerable to both preemption and the threat of unauthorized use. Moreover, the doctrine governing the use of U.S. TNW in Europe is incongruent with the character of the weapons themselves.

These and other weaknesses of the present posture do not, however, appear to have diminished the great political importance of deployed U.S. TNW to Europeans, for whom a U.S. nuclear presence on the continent (although not necessarily the current deployment) represents the most visible proof of the U.S. strategic guarantee. Indeed, the deployment's psychological value within NATO far outweighs whatever military contribution the weapons may make to overall deterrence of aggression from without. Changes in the present posture, therefore, as well as the manner in which they are carried out, must not jeopardize the continuing confidence of Western Europeans in American pledges to defend them. That is, proposals that in European eyes would effectively detach the U.S. strategic deterrent from continental defense—for example, by removing all U.S. TNW from Europe (Alternative 4) or by deploying new weapons deliberately designed not to raise the specter of escalation (the miniaturization option discussed in Alternative 3)—should be avoided.

On the other hand, proposals to reduce the number of deployed TNW

(Alternative 1), to eliminate particularly vulnerable TNW while improving the control over and protection of remaining systems (Alternative 2), and to reduce excessive yields in the existing stockpile seem both desirable and politically feasible. Moreover, their realization would not require significant modifications in present NATO strategy and might effect slight net budgetary savings, while achieving a more manageable and less destabilizing U.S. TNW deployment in Europe.

Based on the foregoing analysis of the current posture and discussion of alternative policies, the author believes the following specific measures should be undertaken:

1. *Reduction of deployed warheads to 2,000.* Such a step would release approximately 25,000 U.S. troops for conventional defense while retaining a TNW deployment in Europe of sufficient redundancy for a major tactical nuclear response to aggression, should one be necessary. The number of warheads to be earmarked for allied use would, of course, be determined through negotiation.

2. *Limitation of warhead yields to not more than 10 kilotons nor less than 0.5 kiloton.* This measure would increase the credibility of the present U.S. TNW stockpile by removing from it warheads of excessive yield. On the other hand, the establishment of a minimum yield of 0.5 kiloton would preserve the integrity of the nuclear threshold by precluding any blurring of the distinction between nuclear and conventional weapons.

3. *Termination of Quick Reaction Alert.* The dropping of QRA would eliminate a highly destabilizing element of present U.S. tactical nuclear posture. It would also increase the number of tactical aircraft available for conventional missions.

4. *Elimination of artillery-delivered nuclear warheads.* This step would remove a relatively vulnerable type of TNW from the deployment and one whose use in time of war would be particularly difficult to control.

5. *Reliance on battlefield and long-range theater missiles as the principal means of delivering tactical nuclear warheads.* Primary reliance on missiles would enhance the stability of the tactical nuclear deterrent by decreasing dependence on tactical aircraft deployed on a relatively small number of exposed airfields. Highly mobile tactical nuclear missile systems such as the *Lance* not only are comparatively invulnerable but also, with the continued development of precision-guidance technology, increasingly capable of performing the nuclear roles now assigned to tactical aircraft and artillery.

94158

The burden of this study has been to establish the necessity for new directions in U.S. tactical nuclear posture in Europe. The author believes that implementation of the above proposals would result in a more credible and rational posture. At a minimum, they represent signposts for further discussion with our allies. The pace and direction of movements toward change thereafter can be judged better in the light of allied reactions to such discussions.

94158